AN
AFRICAN
PRAYER
BOOK

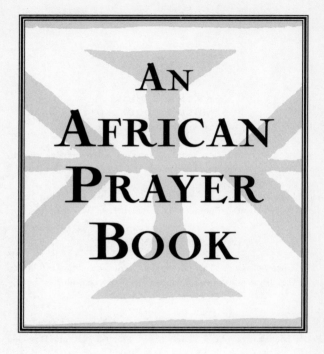

AN AFRICAN PRAYER BOOK

Selected and with Introductions by
Desmond Tutu

IMAGE / DOUBLEDAY
New York London Toronto
Sydney Auckland

AN IMAGE BOOK
PUBLISHED BY DOUBLEDAY
a division of Random House, Inc.

IMAGE, DOUBLEDAY, and the portrayal of a deer drinking from a
stream are registered trademarks of Random House, Inc.

Grateful acknowledgment is made for permission to use lyrics from "Precious
Lord, Take My Hand" by Thomas A. Dorsey, copyright Warner Brothers, Inc.

Book design by Jennifer Ann Daddio

The Library of Congress has cataloged the hardcover edition as follows:
The African prayer book / selected and with an introduction by
Desmond Tutu. — 1st ed.
p.   cm.
1. Africa—Religious life and customs.   2. Christians—Africa—
Prayer-books and devotions—English.   3. Prayers.   I. Tutu, Desmond.
BR1360.A54   1995
242'.8'0096—dc20   94-43444
CIP

ISBN 0-385-51649-5

PRINTED IN THE UNITED STATES OF AMERICA

1   3   5   7   9   10   8   6   4   2

Contents

AN
AFRICAN PRAYER BOOK

INTRODUCTION

Adam was having the time of his life in the Garden of Eden. He enjoyed his work as the primal gardener. The animals loved him and lived in an idyllic, undisturbed harmony. Everything was lovely in the garden. No, not quite. God looked on his human creature and was concerned, for his life was not all unalloyed bliss. God said, "It is not good for man to be alone." And so God asked Adam to choose a mate for himself from among the animals which paraded before him in procession. God would ask his human friend: "What about this one?" Adam would reply: "Not on your life! No, thank you!" And so God decided to put Adam to sleep and produced from his rib that delectable creature, Eve; and when Adam awoke he exclaimed: "Wow! This is just what the doctor ordered."

This beautiful story tells a fundamental truth about us—that we are made to live in a delicate network of interdependence with one another, with God and with the rest of God's creation. We say in our African idiom: "A person is a person through other persons." A solitary human being is a contradiction in terms. A totally self-sufficient human being is ultimately subhuman. We are made for complementarity. I have gifts that you do not; and you have gifts that I do not. *Voilà!* So we need each other to become fully human.

This is also true of the different nations: that one people has particular gifts, a distinct world view, a cultural ethos, which is not necessarily better or superior to those of other people. It is just different and needs to be balanced by those of other peoples. So we find, for instance, that Africans have a strong sense of community, of belonging, whereas Occidentals have in contrast a strong sense of the individual person. These attributes, in isolation and pushed to extremes, have weaknesses. For instance, a strong herd instinct can smother individual initiative so that the person is often sacrificed for the collective, whereas a too highly developed individualism can lead to a debilitating sense of isolation so that you can be lonely and lost in a crowd.

God is smart, making us different so that we will get to know our need of one another. We are meant to complement one another in order to be truly human and to realize the fullness of our potential to be human. After all, we are created in the image of a God who is a diversity of persons who exist in ineffable unity.

This AFRICAN PRAYER BOOK seeks to provide examples of African Christian and non-Christian spirituality with prayers, poems, litanies, songs, acts of adoration, of thanksgiving and supplication and confession, arrow prayers, blessings and even maledictions, as well as acts of dedication and commitment, together with appropriate quotations from the Bible that belong to us all. The composers of the African pieces are in the main Africans, black and white. One or two pieces are by Europeans who have had a deep connection with Africa. We have included compositions from the African diaspora in the United States of America and the West Indies. Although the selection is necessarily subjective I hope that the anthology will not be entirely idiosyncratic and that its appeal will be reasonably catholic and will help many in their prayer lives. Those prayers which seem bound to some time and place can be adapted by modifying specific references.

We used to be taught that properly our prayer should consist of Adoration, Contrition, Thanksgiving and Supplication (the acronym being ACTS) and so the prayers are arranged in sections reflecting this traditional division. The final section, Daily Life, includes prayers that do not easily fall into any one of the prior sections and that relate to aspects of everyday living. You will notice that each of these sections begins with a scriptural passage that shows some of the Bible's encounters with Africa.

We are a remarkable paradox—the finite made for the infinite, the time-bound with a nostalgia for the transcendent, the eternal. It has been said that we each have in us a God-shaped space and only God can fill it. Our natural milieu is the divine and that is why one great African saint and Father of the Church, Augustine of Hippo, could assert in words that are widely quoted:

> Thou hast made us for thyself and our hearts
> are restless until they find their rest in thee.

Whenever we look to find our *summum bonum*— our ultimate good—in anything less than God we are desolated to find that it almost always turns to ashes in our mouths. Whether it be material prosperity, success, drugs, alcohol, sex, exalted into a god, it turns into a demon that leads us to all kinds of perdition.

The African world view rejects the popular dichotomies between the sacred and the secular, the material and the spiritual. All life is religious, all life is sacred, all life is of a piece. The spiritual is real and permeates all existence so that the ancestral spirits, the living dead, are all around us, concerned to promote the well-being of those who are bound together with them in the bundle of life. They are the guardians of morality to ensure that the essential harmony of the community remains intact.

And so before you partake of a drink you spill a little as a libation to acknowledge the presence of this ever present cloud of witnesses surrounding the living and the yet to be born.

There is a lovely prayer of a fisherman who, concerned not to be too harsh in exploiting the river, asks for its permission to fish. What a reverent attitude toward creation. I love the prayer of a dying man. How could we tell that in fact he was not Christian? The encounter with the transcendent reality we call God evokes human responses that are universal.

Our relationship with God is a love affair and ultimately the greatest joy is just to be with the Beloved, to drink in the beauty of the Beloved in a silence that will become ever more wordless and imageless—the silence of just being together. Julian of Norwich said, "Prayer is yearning, beseeching and beholding." We seek to give ourselves to the One who first gave himself to us, this eternally self-giving and self-emptying kenotic One. May God grant that we will all grow in that intimacy that enables us to know we are loved with a love that will never let us go.

As we seek to be like Mary, the sister of Martha, choosing the best part, we will be still in the presence of the One who was God in the beginning and always. God is fullness of beatitude from all eternity, needing nothing outside God in order to be God. God in the most holy trinity is a furnace of love, the Father for ever emptying his whole being to the Son who, coequal and coeternal with the Father, returns this ineffable divine self-empty-ing in an answering kenosis, from all eternity unto the ages of ages. Amen. The love that passes and passed be-tween the Father and the Son is God the Holy Spirit.

Wonderfully, God created us because God *wanted* us, not because God *needed* us. God is absolutely neces-sary, being the Source of all there is. We and everything else that exist are radically contingent. We need never have been. We are like the baby in the womb, utterly and radically dependent on its mother.

We were created by love, for love and so that we should love. "Before I formed you in the womb, I knew you," is what God said to Jeremiah. These are words that apply to each of us. We were planned for from all eter-nity. None of us is a mere divine afterthought. None of us is an accident. *Before the foundation of the world* God chose us to be his children in Jesus Christ. We were loved, that is why we were created. God created you be-cause God loved you. You do not therefore need to do anything to earn or deserve God's love. You do not need to impress God so that God will love you. God already loves you and God will love you for ever and ever. There is nothing you can do that will make God love you less. There is nothing you can do to make God love you more. God's love for you is infinite, perfect and eternal. Tremendous stuff.

And so, as we keep still in the presence of God, we luxuriate in this knowledge: that we are loved, that all we are, all we have is a gift, freely and generously bestowed.

All we must do is to be deeply thankful, to be eucharistic people, to say forever: "Thank you, God, for loving me so much."

Western spirituality illumines some of what I have tried to say. From the "Cloud of Unknowing," hear these beautiful words:

> But now thou askest me and sayest: "How shall I think on himself, and what is he?" Unto this I cannot answer thee, except to say: "I know not."
>
> For thou hast brought me with thy question into that same darkness, and into that same *cloud of unknowing*, that I would thou wert in thyself. For of all other creatures and their works—yea, and of the works of God himself—may a man through grace have fullness of knowing, and well can he think of them; but of God himself can no man think. And therefore I would leave all that thing that I can think, and choose to my love that thing that I cannot think. For why, he may well be loved, but not thought. By love may he be gotten and holden; but by thought never. And therefore, although it be good sometime to think on the kindness and worthiness of God in special, and although it be a light and a part of contemplation: nevertheless in this work it shall be cast down and cov-

ered with a *cloud of forgetting*. And thou shalt step above it stalwartly, but listily, with a devout and a pleasing stirring of love, and try to pierce that darkness above thee. And smite upon that thick *cloud of unknowing* with a sharp dart of longing love; and go not thence for aught that befalleth.

Let these prayers help you to become ever more and more fully what you already are: a child of God, known by name and whose very hairs are numbered. Praise and adore God and thank him for ever and ever. Amen.

Let Saint Augustine have the last word:

All shall be Amen and Alleluia.
We shall rest and we shall see,
We shall see and we shall know,
We shall know and we shall love,
We shall love and we shall praise.
Behold our end which is no end.

AN
AFRICAN
PRAYER
BOOK

ADORATION

All of us are by nature worshipful. We may worship God to whom we ascribe his due, his worth. That is true worship. Or, we may give a false worship to money, to status, etc. When we listen to a superb Beethoven symphony, or something out of Handel's *Messiah*, we are often speechless with wonder and awe. Are we not often awestruck before the grandeur of some imposing mountain range, or when we behold a glorious sunset, or a still, moonlit night with the stars winking in a dark blue sky? I once heard a venerable professor of gynecology, who must have delivered countless babies, confess that he was always overwhelmed by the wonder and mystery of a baby being born. I have heard that scientists wax ecstatic and break into poetic utterance because of the aesthetic qualities of some scientific experiment and the truth that it will have proven. Archimedes ran naked out of his bath when a new scientific truth struck him, shouting "Eureka, eureka" ("I have found it!") In the presence of a good and holy person most of us will be overcome with awe. Standing near Mother Teresa, or Helder Camara, or Nelson Mandela, or Mahatma Gandhi, you know you are standing on holy ground.

On such occasions words are often so utterly inadequate. The story goes of a farmer who used to sit in church for long periods of silence. When he was asked about this practice, he said of our Lord, "I look at him and he looks at me and it is enough." We too have moments when we are struck speechless, as when we are stunned by the beauty of the snowcapped Mt. Kilimanjaro in Tanzania, or the majestic roar of the Victoria Falls in Zimbabwe. Our instinctive worshipfulness then comes to the fore with all these created things; how much more when we encounter the Source of it all—God, who is Beauty, Truth and Goodness? Then we want to fall down to worship and adore the one whose glory fills the heavens and the earth. "Holy, holy, holy is the Lord of hosts."

> O all ye big things of the earth
>   bless ye the Lord . . .
> . . . all ye small things bless ye the Lord . . .

Isn't that beautiful?

> All shall be Amen and Alleluia.
> We shall rest and we shall see,
> We shall see and we shall know,
> We shall know and we shall love,
> We shall love and we shall praise.
> Behold our end which is no end.

Somebody remarked that our praise will not end, because we will for ever discover new aspects of God's beauty, holiness and goodness; for God is infinite, and we are and will always be finite, and so we will be "lost" in wonder, love and praise, as the hymn puts it.

In adoration we begin where we should—with God—by putting first things first. Our Lord taught his disciples a special prayer and it began with God, "Our Father," and then proceeds to glorify and adore him: "hallowed be thy name." In starting with adoration, we follow the pattern our Lord left us.

The day of Pentecost had come, and they were all together in one place. Suddenly there came from the sky what sounded like a strong, driving wind, a noise which filled the whole house where they were sitting. And there appeared to them flames like tongues of fire distributed among them and coming to rest on each one. They were all filled with the Holy Spirit and began to talk in other tongues, as the Spirit gave them power of utterance.

Now there were staying in Jerusalem devout Jews drawn from every nation under heaven. At this sound a crowd of them gathered, and were bewildered because each one heard his own language spoken; they were amazed and in astonishment exclaimed, "Surely these people who are speaking are all Galileans! How is it that each of us can hear them in his own native language? Parthians, Medes, Elamites; inhabitants of Mesopotamia, of Judaea and Cappadocia, of Pontus and Asia, of Phrygia and Pamphylia, of Egypt and the districts of Libya around Cyrene; visitors from Rome, both Jews and proselytes; Cretans and Arabs—all of us hear them telling in our own tongues the great things God has done."

ACTS 2:1–11

AN AFRICAN CANTICLE

All you *big* things, bless the Lord.
Mount Kilimanjaro and Lake Victoria,
The Rift Valley and the Serengeti Plain,

Fat baobabs and shady mango trees,
All eucalyptus and tamarind trees,
Bless the Lord.
Praise and extol Him for ever and ever.

All you *tiny* things, bless the Lord.
Busy black ants and hopping fleas,
Wriggling tadpoles and mosquito larvae,
Flying locusts and water drops,
Pollen dust and tsetse flies,
Millet seeds and dried dagaa,
Bless the Lord.
Praise and extol Him for ever and ever.

TRADITIONAL AFRICAN

TODAY IS GOD

In the beginning was God,
Today is God,
Tomorrow will be God.
Who can make an image of God?
He has no body.
He is the word which comes out of your mouth.
That word! It is no more,
It is past, and still it lives!
So is God.

PYGMY

PRAISE FROM EVERY NATION

After that I looked and saw a vast throng, which no one could count, from all races and tribes, nations and languages, standing before the throne and the Lamb. They were robed in white and had palm branches in their hands, and they shouted aloud:

"Victory to our God who sits on the throne, and to the Lamb!"

All the angels who stood round the throne and round the elders and the four living creatures prostrated themselves before the throne and worshipped God, crying:

"Amen! Praise and glory and wisdom, thanksgiving and honour, power and might, be to our God for ever! Amen."

REVELATION 7:9–12

HOW GREAT THOU ART

Great art thou, O Lord, and greatly to be praised. Great is thy power and thy wisdom is infinite. And thee would man praise, man but a particle of thy creation, man that bears about him his mortality, the witness of his sin, that thou resistest the proud. Yet would man praise thee, he but a particle of thy creation. Thou awakenest us to delight in thy praise. For thou madest us for thyself and our heart is restless until it rest in thee. Grant me, Lord, to know and understand which is first—to call on thee or to praise thee? And again, to know thee or to call on thee? For who can call on thee, not knowing thee? For he that knoweth thee not may call on thee as other than thou art. Or is it better that we call on thee that we may know thee?

SAINT AUGUSTINE

Saint Augustine was the greatest theologian of Western Christianity during its first five centuries. A notable sinner (who described his early life in his autobiographical masterpiece, the Confessions) *he became bishop of Hippo, the second city of Roman Africa, which he served brilliantly till his death in 430.*

LOVE EVER BURNING

O love ever burning and never extinguished charity
My God set me on fire.

SAINT AUGUSTINE

GREAT SPIRIT!

Great Spirit!
Piler-up of the rocks into towering mountains!

When you stamp on the stones
the dust rises and fills the land.
Hardness of the cliff,
waters of the pool that turn
into misty rain when stirred.
Gourd overflowing with oil!
Creator . . . who sews the heavens together like
    cloth,
knit together everything here on the earth below.
You are the one who calls the branching trees into
    life;
you make new seeds grow out of the ground
so that they stand straight and strong.
You have filled the land with people.

Wonderful one, you live
among the sheltering rocks.
You give rain to us people.
We pray to you,
hear us, O Strong One!
When we beg you, show your mercy.
You are in the highest places
with the spirits of the great ones.
You raise the grass-covered hills
above the earth,
and you make the rivers.
Gracious one!

ROZWI, SOUTH AFRICA

GREAT SHIELD

Thou art the great God—the one who is in heaven.
It is thou, thou Shield of Truth,
it is thou, thou Tower of Truth,
it is thou, thou Bush of Truth,
it is thou, thou who sittest in the highest,
thou art the creator of life,
thou madest the regions above.
The creator who madest the heavens also,
the maker of the stars and the Pleiades—
the shooting stars declare it unto us.
The maker of the blind, of thine own will didst thou
    make them.
The trumpet speaks—for us it calls,
Thou art the Hunter who hunts for souls.
Thou art the Leader who goes before us,
thou art the Great Mantle which covers us.
Thou art he whose hands are wounded;
thou art he whose feet are wounded;
thou art he whose blood is a trickling stream—and
    why?
Thou art he whose blood was spilled for us.
For this great price we call,
for thine own place we call.

XHOSA, SOUTH AFRICA

GREAT IS OUR HAPPINESS

Great is, O King,
our happiness
in thy kingdom,
thou, our king.

We dance before thee,
our king,
by the strength
of thy kingdom.

May our feet
be made strong;
let us dance before thee,
eternal.

Give ye praise,
all angels,
to him above
who is worthy of praise.

ZULU, SOUTH AFRICA

I HAVE NO WORDS TO THANK YOU

O my Father, Great Elder,
I have no words to thank you,
But with your deep wisdom
I am sure that you can see
How I value your glorious gifts.
O my Father, when I look upon your greatness,
I am confounded with awe.
O Great Elder,
Ruler of all things earthly and heavenly,
I am your warrior,
Ready to act in accordance with your will.

KIKUYU, KENYA

SEVEN ARCHANGELS

Seven archangels stand glorifying the Almighty and serving the hidden mystery.
Michael the first, Gabriel the second, and Raphael the third, symbol of the Trinity.
Surael, Sakakael, Saratael and Ananael. These are the shining ones, the great and pure ones, who pray to God for mankind.
The cherubim, the seraphim, the thrones, dominions,

powers, and the four living creatures bearing the chariot of God.

The twenty-four elders in the Church of the Firstborn, praise him without ceasing, crying out and saying:

Holy is God; heal the sick. Holy is the Almighty; give rest to the departed. Holy is the Immortal; bless thine inheritance. May thy mercy and thy peace be a stronghold unto thy people.

Holy, holy, holy, Lord of hosts. Heaven and earth are full of thy glory. Intercede for us, O angels our guardians, and all heavenly hosts, that our sins may be forgiven.

COPTIC ORTHODOX

HYMN TO THE BLESSED VIRGIN

O my Lady, the holy Virgin Mary, thou hast been likened to many things, yet there is nothing which compares with thee. Neither heaven can match thee, nor the earth equal as much as the measure of thy womb. For thou didst confine the Unconfinable, and carry him whom none has power to sustain.

The cherubim are but thy Son's chariot bearers, and even the seraphim bow down in homage at the throne of thy Firstborn. How sublime is the honor of thy royal estate.

O holy Virgin, instrument of our strength and power, our grace, deification, joy, and fortune; glory of our human race! Thou wast the means whereby the salvation of the world was accomplished, and through whom God was reconciled to the sons of mankind. And it was through thee that created human nature was united in indivisible union with the Divine Being of the Creator.

What an unheard-of thing for the potter to clothe himself in a clay vessel, or the craftsman in a handicraft. What humility beyond words for the Creator to clothe himself in the body of a human creature.

And now I cry unto thy Son, O Virgin, saying:

O thou who hast preferred the humble estate of men to the high rank of angels, do not reject thy servant because of the sins I have committed.

Thou whose desire was to partake of earthly rather than heavenly beings, let me share in the secret of thy flawless Divine Being.

Thou to whom Jacob was more comely than Esau, do not scorn me because of my transgressions. For against thee only have I sinned, and much sin have I heaped up upon me.

Thou didst create me pure and righteous, yet of my own will I became unclean, and through the persuasion of the wicked one went astray. Thou didst adorn me with gifts of priceless worth which I cast away in favor of unrighteousness.

Make speed, O Lord, to build me into a fortress for the Holy Spirit, Raise me up lest I crumble into a desolate ruin of sin. Make speed to forgive for forgiveness is with thee.

O Lord, thou knowest the balm to heal my wounds, the help to strengthen my weakness, the path to prosper my progress. Thou knowest all that is expedient to fulfil my life, as the potter knows how to contrive his own vessel's perfection. For the work is wrought according to the design and wisdom of its maker.

O Lord, renew thy vessel with the power of the Holy Spirit. Make the work of thy hands to be lovely and indestructible.

O Lord, remember thy descent from the heights of Heaven and thine indwelling within the womb of the Holy Virgin.

Remember thy birth from her while she was a virgin, and the suckling of her who wast chaste.

Remember how thou wast laid in a manger, wrapped in swaddling clothes, in a stable.

O Lord remembering all this, do not disregard thy sinful servant. Help me with thy deliverance and cover me with the shield of thy salvation for the sake of Mary thy

Mother; for the sake of her breasts which suckled thee and her lips which kissed thee; for the sake of her hands which touched thee and her arms which embraced thee; for the sake of her spirit and flesh which thou didst take from her to be part of thyself . . .

I believe, O Lord, that thou art the Son of the Father in thy Godhead, and the Son of Man in thy humanity . . .

I believe, O Lord, that thou art the Firstborn Only Son to him who begat thee and the only Son of her who gave birth to thee. Thy birth in Heaven was unique, and thy birth on earth was unique.

I have sought but could not comprehend the mystery of thy first birth. I contemplate thy second birth and marvel in wonder. I give glory to the former though it is beyond my understanding. I give homage to the second in prostrate adoration.

And now without doubt, and in the fullness of faith, I glorify thy birth from the Father and give praise to thy birth from the Virgin. The Virgin's womb is greater than the mystical chariot of light, loftier than the heights of the firmament, more sublime than the distances of space, more glorious than the seraphim and cherubim.

The Virgin's womb was the gateway to Heaven, which, without being opened, became the way in and way out of the Son of Righteousness . . . The Virgin's womb was the ark and dwelling-place of the Lord God Adonay.

And now let us praise God, saying: Glory to thee; glory to him who sent thee; and glory to the Holy Spirit who is co-equal with thee.

Honor to her who bore thee; homage to her who gave birth to thee; devotion to thy mother; and holiness to her who tended thee.

ETHIOPIAN ORTHODOX

PHARAOH'S HYMN TO THE SUN

Creator of the germ in woman,
Maker of seed in man,
Giving life to the son in the body of his mother,
Soothing him that he may not weep,
Nurse (even) in the womb,
Giver of breath to animate every one that he maketh!
When he cometh forth from the womb . . . on the
    day of his birth,
Thou openest his mouth in speech,
Thou suppliest his necessities.
When the fledgling in the egg chirps in the shell
Thou givest him breath therein to preserve him
    alive. . . .
He goeth about upon his two feet
When he hath come forth therefrom.

How manifold are thy works!
They are hidden from before us
O sole God, whose powers no other possesseth.
Thou didst create the earth according to thy heart.

IKHNATON, 14TH CENTURY B.C.

CHORDS OF PRAISE

I shall sing a song of praise to God:
Strike the chords upon the drum.
God who gives us all good things—
Strike the chords upon the drum—
Wives, and wealth, and wisdom.
Strike the chords upon the drum.

BALUBA, ZAIRE

TRYING TO COUNT THE WAVES

Through death immortality has come to all, and through
the incarnation of the Word God's universal providence
has been made known, together with him who is the
giver and artificer of this providence, God the Word himself. For he became man that we might be made god; and

he revealed himself through a body that we might receive an idea of the unseen Father; and he endured humiliation at men's hands that we might inherit incorruption. In himself he was in no way injured, for he is impassible and incorruptible, the very Word and God; but he endured these things for the sake of suffering men, and through his own impassibility he preserved and saved them. In short, the victories achieved by the Saviour through his incarnation are so great and so many that, if one wished to describe them, it would be like gazing across the open sea and trying to count the waves.

SAINT ATHANASIUS

Athanasius, archbishop of the African city of Alexandria during the fourth century, was called the Champion of Orthodoxy by his devoted people. The great defender of Christ's divinity against the Arians, who wished to reduce him to merely human status, Athanasius was much persecuted, spending many years in exile in the Egyptian desert.

WHEN GOD CREATED ALL THINGS

In the time when God created all things,
God created the sun;
and the sun is born and dies and comes again.
God created the moon;
and the moon is born and dies and comes again.
God created the stars;

and the stars are born and die and come again.
God created humankind;
and a human being is born and dies . . . and does
    not come again.

DINKA, SUDAN

A FISHERMAN'S SONG OF PRAISE

Lord, I sing your praise
the whole day through, until the night.
Dad's nets are filled; I have helped him.
We have drawn them in, stamping the rhythm with
    our feet,
the muscles tense.
We have sung your praise.

On the beach there were our mammies,
who bought the blessings out of the nets,
out of the nets and into their basins.
They rushed to the market, returned and bought
    again.
Lord, what a blessing is the sea, with fish in plenty.
Lord, that is the story of your grace:
nets tear, and we succumb because we cannot hold
    them.
Lord, with your praise we drop off to sleep.
Carry us through the night.

Make us fresh for the morning.
Halleluiah for the day!
And blessing for the night! Amen.

GHANA

A DIVINE INVOCATION

O God, Framer of the universe, grant me first
rightly to invoke thee; then to show myself worthy
to be heard by thee; lastly, deign to set me free.
God, through whom all things, which of themselves were
not, tend to be. God, who withholdest from perishing
even that which seems to be mutually destructive. God,
who, out of nothing, hast created this world, which the
eyes of all perceive to be most beautiful. God, who dost
not cause evil, but causest that it be not most evil. God,
who to the few that flee for refuge to that which truly is,
showest evil to be nothing. God, through whom the universe, even taking in its sinister side, is perfect. God,
from whom things most widely at variance with thee ef-
fect no dissonance, since worser things are included in
one plan with better. God, who art loved, wittingly or
unwittingly, by everything that is capable of loving. God,
in whom are all things, to whom nevertheless neither the
vileness of any creature is vile, nor its wickedness harm-
ful, nor its error erroneous. God, who hast not willed

that any but the pure should know the truth. God, the Father of truth, the Father of wisdom, the Father of the true and crowning life, the Father of blessedness, the Father of that which is good and fair, the Father of intelligible light, the Father of our awakening and illumination, the Father of the pledge by which we are admonished to return to thee.

Thee I invoke, O God, the Truth, in whom and from whom and through whom all things are true which anywhere are true. God, the Wisdom, in whom and from whom and through whom all things are wise which anywhere are wise. God, the true and crowning Life, in whom and from whom and through whom all things live which truly and supremely live. God, the Blessedness, in whom and from whom and through whom all things are blessed which anywhere are blessed. God, the Good and Fair, in whom and from whom and through whom all things are good and fair which anywhere are good and fair. God, the intelligible Light, in whom and from whom and through whom all things intelligibly shine which anywhere intelligibly shine. God, whose kingdom is that whole world of which sense has no ken. God, from whose kingdom a law is even derived down upon these lower realms. God, from whom to be turned away is to fall: to whom to be turned back is to rise again: in whom to abide is to stand firm. God, from whom to go forth is to die: to whom to return is to revive: in whom to have our dwelling is to live. God, whom no one loses, unless deceived: whom no one seeks, unless stirred up: whom no one finds, unless made pure. God, whom to forsake is one thing with perishing; toward whom to tend is one thing with loving: whom to see is one thing with having. God, toward whom faith rouses us, hope lifts us up, with whom love joins us. God, through whom we overcome the enemy, thee I entreat. God, through whose gift it is that we do not perish utterly. God, by whom we are warned to watch. God, by whom we distinguish good from ill. God, by whom we flee evil and follow good. God, through whom we yield not to calamities. God, through whom we faithfully serve and benignantly govern. God, through whom we learn those things to be another's which aforetime we accounted ours, and those things to be ours which we used to account as belonging to another. God, through whom the baits and enticements of evil things have no power to hold us. God, through whom it is that diminished possessions leave ourselves complete. God, through whom our better good is not subject to a worse. God, through whom death is swallowed up in victory. God, who dost turn us to thyself. God, who dost strip us of that which is not, and arrayest us in that which is. God, who dost make us worthy to be heard. God, who dost fortify us. God, who leadest us into all truth. God, who speakest to us only good, who neither terrifiest into madness or sufferest another so to do. God, who callest us back into the way. God, who leadest us to the door of life. God, who causest it to be opened to them that knock. God, who givest us the bread of life. God, through whom we thirst for the draught, which being drunk we never thirst. God, who dost convince the world of sin, of righteousness, and of judgment. God, through whom it is that we are not commoved by those who refuse to believe. God, through whom we disapprove the error of those who think that there are no merits of souls before thee. God, through whom it comes that we are not in bondage to the weak and beggarly elements. God, who cleansest us and pre-parest us for divine rewards, to me propitious come thou.

Whatever has been said by me, thou the only God, do thou come to my help, the one true and eternal substance, where is no discord, no confusion, no shifting, no indigence, no death. Where is supreme con-cord, supreme evidence, supreme steadfastness, supreme fullness, and life supreme. Where nothing is lacking, nothing redundant. Where Begetter and Begotten are one. God, whom all things serve that serve, to whom is compliant every virtuous soul. By whose laws the poles revolve, the stars fulfill their courses, the sun vivifies the day, the moon tempers the night: and all the framework of things, day after day by vicissitude of light and gloom, month after month by waxings and wanings of the moon, year after year by orderly successions of spring and sum-mer and fall and winter, cycle after cycle by accom-plished concurrences of the solar course, and through the mighty orbs of time, folding and refolding upon them-selves, as the stars still recur to their first conjunctions, maintains, so far as this merely visible matter allows, the mighty constancy of things. God, by whose ever-during laws the stable motion of shifting things is suffered to feel no perturbation, the thronging course of circling ages is ever recalled anew to the image of immovable quiet; by whose laws the choice of the soul is free, and to the good rewards and to the evil pains are distributed by necessities settled throughout the nature of everything. God, from whom distill even to us all benefits, by whom all evils are withheld from us. God, above whom is nothing, beyond whom is nothing, without whom is nothing. God, under whom is the whole, in whom is the whole, with whom is the whole. Who hast made man after thine image and likeness, which he discovers who has come to know himself. Hear me, hear me, graciously hear me, my God, my Lord, my King, my Father, my Cause, my Hope, my Wealth, my Honor, my House, my Country, my Health, my Light, my Life. Hear, hear, hear me graciously, in that way, all thine own, which though known to few is to those few known so well.

Henceforth thee alone do I love, thee alone I follow, thee alone I seek, thee alone am I prepared to serve, for thou alone art Lord by a just title, of thy dominion do I desire to be. Direct, I pray, and command whatever thou wilt, but heal and open my ears that I may hear thine utterances. Heal and open my eyes that I may behold thy significations of command. Drive delusion from me that I may recognize thee. Tell me whither I must tend, to behold thee, and I hope that I shall do all things thou mayest enjoin. O Lord, most merciful Father, receive, I pray, thy fugitive; enough already, surely, have I been punished, long enough have I served thine enemies, whom thou hast under thy feet, long enough have I been a sport of fallacies. Receive me fleeing from these, thy house-born servant, for did not these receive me, though another master's, when I was fleeing from thee? To thee I feel I must return: I knock; may thy door be opened to me; teach me the way to thee. Nothing else have I than the will: nothing else do I know than that fleeting and falling things are to be spurned, fixed and everlasting things to be sought. This I do, Father, because this alone I know, but from what quarter to approach thee I do not know. Do thou instruct me, show me, give me my provision for the way. If it is by faith that those find thee who take refuge with thee, then grant faith: if by virtue, virtue: if by knowledge, knowledge. Augment in me faith, hope, and charity. O goodness of thine, singular and most to be admired!

I beseech thee and once again I beg of thee the means to beseech thee. For if thou abandon me, I perish: but thou dost not abandon me because thou art the Supreme Good whom no one ever sought with justice and could not discover. And all have sought thee rightly to whom thou hast given to seek thee rightly. Grant me, Father, that I may seek thee; keep me from error. Let me find none but thee when I seek thee. I beg thee, Father. But if I have in me any trace of desire, do thou make me clean and fit to behold thee. And with regard to the health of this my mortal body, so long as I do not know what advantage it has for me, or those whom I love, I commit it to thee, Father, most wise and most good; and I shall pray for it when thou dost advise me. Only this I beg of thy exceeding mercy—that thou turnest me wholly to thee and grantest that nothing stand in my way when I come to thee. And do thou command me, so long as I move and wear this body, that I be pure and high of soul and just and prudent, that I be the perfect lover and perceiver of thy wisdom and worthy of thy dwelling place; and grant me to dwell in thy most blessed kingdom. Amen. Amen.

SAINT AUGUSTINE

THE SOURCE OF BEING IS ABOVE

The source of being is above,
which gives life to all people;
For people are satisfied, and do not die of famine,
For the Lord gives them life,
that they may live prosperously
on the earth and not die of famine.

ZULU, SOUTH AFRICA

THE GREAT AMEN

Asithi—Amen, siyakudumisa,
Asithi—Amen, siyakudumisa,
Asithi—Amen, Baba, Amen, Baba,
Amen, siyakudumisa.

Amen, amen—Amen, praise the name of the Lord,
Amen, amen—Amen, praise the name of the Lord,
Amen, amen—Amen, amen, Amen, amen,
Amen, praise the name of the Lord.

ZULU, SOUTH AFRICA

MORNING PRAISE

To thee, O Master that lovest all men, I hasten on rising
from sleep; by thy mercy I go forth to do thy work, and
I pray to thee: help me at all times, in everything; deliver
me from every evil thing of this world and from every attack of the devil; save me and bring me to thine eternal
kingdom. For thou art my Creator, the Giver and Pro-
vider of everything good; in thee is all my hope, and to
thee I ascribe glory, now and ever, and to the ages of ages.
Amen.

SAINT MACARIUS

SILENCE ALIVE

Silent Father
Silent Son
Silent Holy Spirit
Silent One——I love you.
In the silence of eyes

                              I see you.

In the silence of unspoken words

                              I hear you.

In the silence of a sudden touch

                              I feel you.

In the silence of a flower's fragrance

                              I smell you.

In the silence of bread and wine

                              I taste you.

Sensual God, I love you!

I love you in the silence——

                              Silent Father
                              Silent Son
                              Silent Holy Spirit
                              Silent One——I love you!

HARRY ALFRED WIGGETT

Harry Alfred Wiggett is an Anglican priest living in the seaside town of Fish Hoek, near Cape Town, where he is rector of St. Margaret's Church.

THE RIGHT HAND OF GOD

The right hand of God is writing in our land,
Writing with power and with love.
Our conflicts and our fears, our triumphs and our
    tears
Are recorded by the right hand of God.

The right hand of God is pointing in our land,
Pointing the way we must go.
So clouded is the way, so easily we stray,
But we're guided by the right hand of God.

The right hand of God is striking in our land,
Striking out at envy, hate and greed.
Our selfishness and lust, our pride and deeds unjust
Are destroyed by the right hand of God.

The right hand of God is lifting in our land,
Lifting the fallen one by one.
Each one is known by name,
And rescued now from shame,
By the lifting of the right hand of God.

The right hand of God is healing in our land,
Healing broken bodies, minds and souls,
So wondrous is its touch,
With love that means so much,
When we're healed by the right hand of God.

The right hand of God is planting in our land,
Planting seeds of freedom, hope and love,
In these Caribbean lands.
Let his people all join hands,
And be one with the right hand of God.

THE CARIBBEAN CONFERENCE OF CHURCHES

AMEN AND ALLELUIA

All shall be Amen and Alleluia.
We shall rest and we shall see,
We shall see and we shall know.
We shall know and we shall love.
We shall love and we shall praise.
Behold our end which is no end.

SAINT AUGUSTINE

CONTRITION

When you have sat for a long time in a darkened room, it is agony to go outside into the unbearable glare of the blazing sun. For a sinner to be in the presence of the all-consuming holiness of God is equally unbearable, indeed impossible. In the *Dream of Gerontius* the soul of Gerontius yearns to be brought before God. But when this does happen, Gerontius cries out, in unspeakable anguish, "Take me away." Sinfulness and holiness cannot coexist.

And so when Isaiah beholds the Lord high and lifted up, with the angelic hosts singing in worship and adoration, "Holy, holy, holy," he becomes so aware of his own unworthiness and sinfulness that he cries out:

> Woe is me, for I am a man of unclean lips, and dwell among a people of unclean lips . . .

Peter, the chief apostle, knelt before Jesus after the miraculous catch of fish and said, "Depart from me for I am a sinner."

We have a paradox here—the holiness and goodness of God both repel and attract. We want to approach and yet we are overawed by the holiness, which repels us. And yet this God in Jesus comes as the friend of sinners who sits at table with tax collectors, prostitutes and sinners whom the world despises. He welcomes his wayward children like the father of the prodigal, who sets aside all his patriarchal dignity as he rushes out to welcome his long-lost son.

He does not stand on ceremony. This God in Jesus

Christ goes after the recalcitrant, troublesome lost sheep, and when he finds this unattractive, smelly rogue, actually bears it joyfully home on his shoulders and has a celebration to mark its finding and return.

Incredibly, but such is the Good News, there is greater joy in heaven over one sinner who repents than over ninety-nine righteous ones who need no repentance. But it is all of a piece with the wonder that makes St. Paul exult, "whilst we were yet sinners, Christ died for us." At the moment when we least deserved it, God demonstrated his gracious love by pouring it out so unreservedly for us. To sin is to hurt and reject this love. Forgiveness is the possibility of a new start. When we fail, God does not abandon us and say, "Good riddance to bad rubbish!" No, God picks us up, dusts us off and says, "Try again." Christianity is the faith of ever-new beginnings. The hardest words in any language are "I am sorry. Please forgive me," and yet they alone can help restore a personal relationship which a wrong has disturbed.

A Jew had a particular besetting sin, and he used to confess it and God would forgive him. But no sooner had he been absolved than he would trip up and sin again. One day this happened and he rushed back to God and said, "I'm sorry, I've done it again." And God asked, "What have you done again?" For God suffers from amnesia when it comes to our sins. God does not look at the caterpillar we are now, but the dazzling butterfly we have it in us to become. In the Lord's Prayer, Jesus bids us ask God to forgive us as we forgive those who have wronged us. Not to forgive others is to shut the door to our own being forgiven.

As they led him away to execution they took hold of a man called Simon, from Cyrene, on his way in from the country; putting the cross on his back they made him carry it behind Jesus.

LUKE 23:26

A LITANY OF CONFESSION

Lord, we confess our day-to-day failure to be human.
  Lord, we confess to you.
Lord, we confess that we often fail to love with all we have and are, often because we do not fully understand what loving means, often because we are afraid of risking ourselves.
  Lord, we confess to you.
Lord, we cut ourselves off from each other and we erect barriers of division.
  Lord, we confess to you.
Lord, we confess that by silence and ill-considered word
  We have built up walls of prejudice.
Lord, we confess that by selfishness and lack of sympathy
  We have stifled generosity and left little time for others.
Holy Spirit, speak to us. Help us to listen to your word of forgiveness, for we are very deaf. Come fill this moment and free us from our sin.

CATHEDRAL CHURCH OF SAINT GEORGE,
CAPE TOWN

An Act of Reconciliation and Sharing of the Peace

Throughout the land we stand on the threshold of a new experience of national unity. We are a people composed of many races, many languages, many religious traditions, many political parties, many cultures. We are poor and rich, women and men, young and old. We have emerged from a history of strife and death to seek a future of life and health.
We acknowledge the presence of Christ amongst us who reconciles the world.

We struggled against one another: now we are reconciled to struggle for one another.
We believed it was right to withstand one another: now we are reconciled to understand one another.
We endured the power of violence: now we are reconciled to the power of tolerance.

We built irreconcilable barriers between us: now we seek to build a society of reconciliation.
We suffered a separateness that did not work: now we are reconciled to make togetherness work.
We believed we alone held the truth: now we are reconciled in the knowledge that truth holds us.

We tried to frighten one another into submission: now we are reconciled to lift one another into fulfillment.

We revered or rejected the apartheid system: now we are reconciled to pray for those set in authority over us.

We fought to call the land our own: now we know reconciliation is in knowing that Earth belongs to God and we are stewards of it.

We let greed control us: now we know reconciliation is measured by the development of the poor.

In Church and State we often hurt each other: now we are reconciled to healing one another.

We set the Church at odds with itself: now we are reconciled to sharing the mission of Christ. We rejected other people of faith as godless: now we are reconciled to seek God's way for us all.

We puffed ourselves up to demand others bow to us: now we are reconciled to embrace one another in humility before God.

We do not pretend we have already won or are already perfect: now we are reconciled to press on together to the fullness which lies ahead.

So we bring together our races, languages, traditions, politics, and cultures.

All: We are all Africans. We commit ourselves to discover an African solution, under God.

We are reconciled to the patience and persistence that make peace; to the transparency and fairness that make justice; to the forgiveness and restitution that build harmony; to the love and reconstruction which banish poverty and discrimination; to the experience of knowing one another that makes it possible to enjoy one another; to the spiritual strength of the one God, who made us of one flesh and blood, and loves us.

Let us share the peace together.

SOUTH AFRICA, NATIONAL SERVICE OF
THANKSGIVING, MAY 8, 1994

O JESUS, MY FEET ARE DIRTY

O Jesus, my feet are dirty. Come even as a slave to me, pour water into your bowl, come and wash my feet. In asking such a thing I know I am overbold but I dread what was threatened when you said to me, "If I do not wash your feet I have no fellowship with you." Wash my feet then, because I long for your companionship. And yet, what am I asking? It was well for Peter to ask you to wash his feet; for him that was all that was needed for him to be clean in every part. With me it is different; though you wash me now I shall still stand in need of that other washing, the cleansing you promised when you said, "There is a baptism I must needs be baptized with."

ORIGEN

Origen, one of the earliest Christian theologians, was born in Africa, probably at Alexandria, toward the end of the second century. He endured terrible tortures for the faith after his arrest in 250 during the Decian persecution. Many of his writings, which provoked great controversy during his lifetime and after his death, have been lost but we know that he was a great scripture scholar who worked to secure a more reliable text of the Old Testament by careful comparison of Hebrew and Greek versions.

A BALM IN GILEAD

There is a balm in Gilead to make the wounded
   whole;
There is a balm in Gilead to heal the sin-sick soul.

Sometimes I feel discouraged,
And think my work's in vain,
But then the Holy Spirit
Revives my soul again.

If you can't preach like Peter,
If you can't pray like Paul,
Just tell the love of Jesus,
And say he died for all.

AFRICAN-AMERICAN SPIRITUAL

You Have Helped My Life to Grow Like a Tree

God in heaven, you have helped my life to grow like a tree. Now something has happened. Satan, like a bird, has carried in one twig of his own choosing after another. Before I knew it he had built a dwelling place and was living in it. Tonight, my Father, I am throwing out both the bird and the nest.

NIGERIA

God Has Turned His Back on Us

God has turned his back on us;
the words of men have made him angry.
And yet he will turn round again.
God has turned his back on us.
We are the children of our Maker
and are not afraid that he will kill us.

DINKA, SUDAN

May Anger and Fear Turn to Love

O God
whose Son in anger
drove the money-changers
from the temple
let the anger of Nkwenkwe Nkomo
and his fellow detainees
be to the cleansing
of this land.

O God
I hold before you
the anger
the rage
the frustration
the sorrow
of Mrs. Nkomo and all black mothers
who demand for their children
the same chance to grow up
strong and tall
loving and unafraid
as any white mother
wants for her children;

In penitence
I offer you
my own mixed-up anger

that it, with theirs,
may be taken up
into your redemptive will
in which the clash
between anger and fear
oppressed and oppressor
can give way
to the incomprehensible action
of agape-love
bringing about the reconciliation
the embrace of the other
the alien
the enemy
creating the festival of shalom
in which the wolf shall lie down
with the lamb
and the whole of life on earth
shall rejoice
in the splendor of your glory.

MARGARET NASH

Dr. Margaret Nash is a prominent Anglican layperson in Cape Town. She joined black workers in resisting the bulldozing of their shacks, which had been declared illegal under apartheid laws. Nkwenkwe Nkomo was one of thousands of young people who were jailed without trial laws during the apartheid era.

Confession of Alexandria

We African Christians gathered from all parts of the continent in the General Committee of the All Africa Conference of Churches, praised God for having brought us together in Alexandria, the holy city in which tradition places the martyrdom of St. Mark, the Evangelist:

Therefore God calls us to repentance
He grants us forgiveness,
He leads us to confess our faith with joy,
in the great fellowship of
the Saints throughout the ages

The Christian Community in Africa gives praise to God for His revelation through Jesus Christ, His Son and His constant presence among His people through the Holy Spirit.

As members of Christ's Church in Africa today, we have become conscious of the fact that we are inheritors of a rich tradition. Our current concern with issues related to:

economic justice
the total liberation of
men and women from every
form of oppression and
exploitation and for
peace in Africa

as well as our contemporary search for authentic responses to Christ as Lord over the whole of our lives has led us to a deeper understanding of the heritage delivered to us by the Fathers of the Early Church in North Africa.

Our commitment to the struggle for human liberation is one of the ways we confess our faith in an incarnate God, who loved us so much that He came among us in our own human form, suffered, was crucified for our redemption and was raised for our justification. Such undeserved grace evokes a response of love and joy that we are seeking to express and to share in language, modes of spirituality, liturgical forms, patterns of mission and structures of organization that belong uniquely to our own cultural context.

This is what the Fathers of the Early Church in North Africa did with the Gospel brought to them by St. Mark. As a result they were able to develop a Christianity that was orthodox and catholic both in its outreach and in its cultural authenticity—and a Church which throughout the ages has endured persecution and martyrdom, and still survives, with renewed strength, until our day.

It is this heritage which inspires us to confess that it is the same Incarnate Christ who is calling us to respond to Him in terms that are authentic, faithful and relevant to the men and women in Africa today. His call is our present and our future.

As this future breaks into the present, Christians in

Africa have every reason to be joyful. Through the continuing work of Christ, God is charting His Highway of Freedom (Isaiah 40:3–5) from Alexandria to the Cape of Good Hope. By witnessing to the victorious power of the Cross (Romans 8) we Christians in Africa are encouraged to be co-workers with all those who are called by God to participate in His work.

The Storms of History have sometimes led us astray. We have been too willing to rush off this Highway into dead-end paths. We have not always kept close around Christ. We have spoken against evil when it was convenient. We have often avoided suffering for the sake of others, thus refusing to follow His example (1 Peter 2:21). We have preferred religiosity to listening to what the Holy Spirit might be whispering to us. We have struggled against colonialism and many other evils and yet have built up again those things which we had torn down (Gal. 2:18). We confess that we have often condoned exploitation and oppression by foreigners. When we have condemned these evils we have condoned the same things by our people. We have turned a blind eye to the structures of injustice in our societies, concentrating on the survival of our churches as institutions.

We have been a stumbling block for too many. For these and many other sins, we are sorry and ask God to forgive us.

A full understanding of this forgiveness leaves us no choice but to continue the struggle for the full liberation of all men and women, and of their societies.

We accept that political liberation in Africa, and the Middle East, is part of this liberation. But the enslaving forces and the abuse of human rights in independent Africa point to the need for a more comprehensive understanding of liberation. Liberation is therefore a CONTINUING STRUGGLE (Lusaka '74).

> *Now to Him who is able to do*
> *immeasurably more than all*
> *we can ask or conceive, by*
> *the power which is at work*
> *among us, to Him be glory in*
> *the Church and in Christ*
> *Jesus from generation to*
> *generation evermore!*

(EPHESIANS 3:20—21)

ALL AFRICA CONFERENCE OF CHURCHES

THANKSGIVING

I have always been intrigued by the story of our Lord's healing of the ten lepers. As they were on their way to show themselves to the priests who would attest to their cure, they were healed. But only one, a despised Samaritan, returned to our Lord to express his gratitude. Our Lord, surprised that only one had done so, then told this Samaritan to rise and go, for his faith had made him whole. It seems odd that Jesus should appear to repeat his cure, since the story had already recorded the healing of all ten. I have thought that perhaps this Gospel story points to a deeper leprosy in the spirit, the leprosy of ingratitude. To be unthankful, to be unappreciative, is in fact to be diseased. To cleanse our spirits of depression, of self-pity and other forms of spiritual leprosy, we have to be thankful, appreciative persons.

There is a song which used to be sung by Sunday school children,

Count your blessings, name them one by one
    And see what God hath done,
Count your blessings, name them one by one
    And it will surprise you what the Lord hath done

It is not great music or impressive poetry, but it teaches a very important lesson.

I love the story of the woman who was a sinner gate-crashing a party where our Lord was a guest. She made an embarrassing spectacle of herself, being in public without a head-covering and weeping over our Lord's feet, kissing them and wiping them with her hair. The host was appalled that Jesus let her continue what he considered her disgraceful conduct when as a prophet he should have known her reputation as a lady of so-called easy virtue. I have always believed this was Mary Magdalene who became the Queen of Penitents. I love her, and she is one of my three patron saints. Jesus, reading his host's mind, points out that Mary was pouring out her love and thanks because she had been forgiven a great deal. Jesus was a deeply thankful person. He thanked God for hiding the divine mystery from the great and wise, and for revealing it to the childlike and simple. He gave thanks over the bread and fish before the miracle of the feeding of the five thousand, and of course he gave thanks over the bread and the wine when he instituted the Eucharist.

Tradition teaches that he thanked the woman who wiped his sweaty face covered in spittle and dried blood when he walked the *Via Dolorosa*; and so Veronica had the true image of Jesus imprinted on her cloth.

At the heart of the Christian life is the Eucharist, the Great Thanksgiving. Saint Augustine of Hippo used to say to his converts "Become what you are" as they shared in the Eucharist, for they were the bread and the wine, the Body and Blood of Christ. They were being exhorted to be eucharistic people, the community that was for ever saying "Thank you" to God for everything; for life, for good health, for food, for safety in travel, for joy, for laughter, for friendship, for fish caught, for a job, for the stars, for the sun, for birds, for grace, for God.

Unless we are thankful, we will suffer the leprosy of ingratitude. We will be depressed and full of self-pity and jealousy.

Then the angel of the Lord said to Philip, "Start out and go south to the road that leads down from Jerusalem to Gaza."(This is the desert road.) He set out and was on his way when he caught sight of an Ethiopian. This man was a eunuch, a high official of the Kandake, or queen, of Ethiopia, in charge of all her treasure; he had been to Jerusalem on a pilgrimage and was now returning home, sitting in his carriage and reading aloud from the prophet Isaiah. The Spirit said to Philip, "Go and meet the carriage." When Philip ran up he heard him reading from the prophet Isaiah and asked, "Do you understand what you are reading?" He said, "How can I without someone to guide me?" and invited Philip to get in and sit beside him.

The passage he was reading was this: "He was led like a sheep to the slaughter; like a lamb that is dumb before the shearer, he does not open his mouth. He has been humiliated and has no redress. Who will be able to speak of his posterity? For he is cut off from the world of the living."

"Please tell me," said the eunuch to Philip, "who it is that the prophet is speaking about here: himself or someone else?" Then Philip began and, starting from this passage, he told him the good news of Jesus. As they were going along the road, they came to some water. "Look," said the eunuch, "here is water: what is to prevent my being baptized?" and he ordered the carriage to stop. Then they both went down into the water, Philip and the eunuch, and he baptized him. When they came up from the water the Spirit snatched Philip away; the eunuch did not see him again, but went on his way rejoicing.

ACTS 8:26—39

THANKFULNESS FOR HOPES FULFILLED

We thank you, O God,
You have answered us.
You have saved us together with our children
here in the place where you put us in your loving
    will.
We praise you, we sing of you, because you watch
    over this
piece of land which is Crossroads.
You, O God, are to be praised
because you never let us fall into the hands of those
who would tear us apart.
O God, may you help us and our children in all our
    needs
just as you did the Israelites in the desert.
Our eyes have seen the evil which reigns over this
    land of ours—South Africa.
We have seen, O Lord, those who call themselves
    Christians,
but who instead are used by Satan.
Enter their hearts and reveal to them the coming
    judgment.
Lord God of hosts, when we have you, we have all
    things.
When our enemies are upon us, we do not fear,
because you said that all who trust in you will not be
    disappointed.

We too, O Lord, have hope that you are present and
supply our need.
You once spoke in the wilderness and stilled the
dangerous snakes.
You have spoken your word even in this wilderness
at Crossroads.
When enemies rose up against us, their strength
failed.
Even death did not defeat us.
Just as David says: the Lord is my shepherd.
Our help is in the name of the Lord. Amen.

CROSSROADS, A SQUATTER COMMUNITY
NEAR CAPE TOWN

A LITANY OF REJOICING

Leader: For rebirth and resilience,
People: Blessed be God;
Leader: For the spiritually humble,
People: Glory to God, hallelujah;
Leader: For all who are hungry and thirsty for justice,
People: Praise him and magnify him forever;
Leader: For all who are banned for speaking the
truth,
People: Blessed be God;

Leader: For all who triumph over their bitter
        circumstance
People: Glory to God, hallelujah!
Leader: For all who risk reputation, livelihood and life
        itself for Christ's sake and the gospel;
People: All praise and all glory; this is God's kingdom;
        praise him and love him forever. Amen.

CAPE TOWN, SOUTH AFRICA

CREATOR OF OUR LAND

O Lord, O God,
creator of our land,
our earth, the trees,
the animals and humans,
all is for your honor.
The drums beat it out,
and people sing about it,
and they dance with noisy joy
that you are the Lord.

You also have pulled the other continents
out of the sea.
What a wonderful world you have made
out of wet mud,
and what beautiful men and women!

We thank you for all the beauty of this earth.
The grace of your creation is like a cool day
between rainy seasons.
We drink in your creation with our eyes.
We listen to the birds' jubilee
with our ears.
How strong and good
and sure your earth smells,
and everything that grows there.

The sky above us
is like a warm, soft Kente cloth,
because you are behind it,
else it would be cold and rough and uncomfortable.
We drink in your creation
and cannot get enough of it.
But in doing this we forget
the evil we have done.

Lord, we call you,
we beg you:
tear us away from our sins
and our death.
This wonderful world fades away.
And one day our eyes snap shut,
and all is over and dead
that is not from you.
We are still slaves of the demons
and the fetishes of this earth,

when we are not saved by you.
Bless us.
Bless our land and people.
Bless our forests with mahogany,
wawa, and cacao.
Bless our fields with cassava and peanuts.
Bless the waters
that flow through our land.
Fill them with fish
and drive great schools of fish to our seacoast,
so that the fishermen in their unsteady boats
do not need to go out too far.
Be with us youth in our countries,
and in all Africa,
and in the whole world.
Prepare us for the service that we should render.

ASHANTI, GHANA

MY JOYS MOUNT AS DO THE BIRDS

Lord, my joys mount as do the birds,
heavenward.
The night has taken wings
and I rejoice in the light.
What a day, Lord! What a day!

Your sun has burned away the dew
from the grass and from our hearts.

What erupts from us,
what encircles us this morning,
is thanksgiving.

Lord, we thank you for all and everything.
Lord, I thank you for what I am,
for my body tall and broad,
despite the meagre meals at school,
and although Father has no work.
This body grows and grows
even with malaria in my blood.

Lord, I also thank you
for this job [on the railway],
which I found during my holidays.
I make good money;
the money for school lies already in Father's trunk.
You can let me advance far, but I know
I can never outdo your trees.

Lord, I am happy this morning.
Birds and angels sing and I am exultant.
The universe and our hearts are open to your grace.
I feel my body and give thanks.
The sun burns my skin and I thank you.
The breakers are rolling toward the seashore,
the sea foam splashes our house.
I give thanks.

Lord, I rejoice in your creation,
and that you are behind it, and before,
and next to it, and above—and within us.

Lord, your sun is balmy,
it caresses the grass and the cassava out of the clay,
tops it with flowers,
draws out the mahogany,
throws birds into the sky,
and out of us it drums
a song of praise for you.

GHANA

THANK YOU VERY MUCH!

Thank you very, very much;
my God, thank you.
Give me food today,
food for my sustenance every day.
Thank you very, very much.

SAMBURU, KENYA

OUR LOVING ETERNAL PARENT

O God our loving Eternal Parent, we praise you with a great shout of joy! Your ruling power has proved victorious! For centuries our land seemed too dark for sunrise, too bloody for healing, too sick for recovery, too hateful for reconciliation. But you have brought us into the daylight of liberation; you have healed us with new hope; you have stirred us to believe our nation can be reborn; we see the eyes of our sisters and brothers shining with resolve to build a new South Africa. Accept our prayers of praise and thanksgiving.

We thank you for our grandmothers and grandfathers who taught us to believe in liberation. We thank you for those who are great names to all our country now: Luthuli, Sobukwe, Biko, Visser, Joseph, Ngoyi, Hani, Tambo, and a thousand others. Many are named with our own names, treasured in our hearts, honored in our memories. Many rest in graves in other lands so that South African love embraces the world. We remember those thousands of people overseas who gave themselves in solidarity that our nation might be changed.

For all of these we thank and praise you. We thank you that democracy has come, and for the wonder of a government of national unity. We thank you for the commitment among all people to seek justice and peace, homes and jobs, education and health, reconciliation and reconstruction. We thank you that because apartheid has gone we can turn from the days of destruction to the work of reconstruction together. For our rich variety, our rich vision and our rich land, we thank you.

We thank you for the spiritual power which gives us new birth. You have given us the courage to change our minds, to open our hearts to those we despised, and to discover we can disagree without being enemies. We are not winners and losers, but citizens who push and pull together to move the nation forward. We thank you for the Good News that you will always be with us, and will always overcome: that love will conquer hatred; that tolerance will conquer antagonism; that cooperation will conquer conflict; that your Holy Spirit can empower our spirits; through Jesus Christ our Lord.

SOUTH AFRICA, NATIONAL SERVICE OF
THANKSGIVING, MAY 1994

OUR CHURCHES ARE LIKE
BIG FAMILIES

Lord, we thank you that our churches are like big families.
Lord, let your spirit of reconciliation blow over all the earth.
Let Christians live your love.
Lord, we praise you in Europe's cathedrals, in America's offerings,

And in our African songs of praise.
Lord, we thank you that we have brothers and sisters
   in all the world.
Be with them that make peace.
Amen.

WEST AFRICA

MOGOPA

Mogopa, a village to the west of Johannesburg, was to be demolished and its inhabitants forcibly removed at gun-point to a homeland in apartheid's forced population-removal schemes. On the eve of their departure, a vigil with Church leaders from all over South Africa was held in Mogopa. The village clinics, shops, schools and churches had already been demolished. At about mid-night an elder of the doomed village got up to pray and he prayed a strange prayer that I will never forget. He said, "God, thank you for loving us so much."

    Several years later, apartheid is dead and the people of Mogopa have returned to their village, which they are rebuilding. God did indeed love them very much, it seems.

A MOGOPA ELDER

ALL ARE KINGS AND PROPHETS

Do you not realize or understand your own nobility?
Each of those who have been anointed with the heavenly
chrism becomes a Christ by grace, so that all are kings
and prophets of the heavenly mysteries.

SAINT MACARIUS

YOU HAVE OUR FAITH WITH
OUR BODIES

Father, thank you for your revelation
    about death
    and illness
    and sorrow.

Thank you for speaking so plainly to us,
    for calling us all friends
    and hovering over us;
    for extending your arms out to us.

We cannot stand on our own;
    we fall into death without you.
    We fall from faith, left to our own.
    We are really friendless without you.

Your extended arms fill us with joy,
    expressing love,
    love caring and carrying,
    asking and receiving our trust.

You have our trust, Father,
    and our faith,
    with our bodies
    and all that we are and possess.

We fear nothing when with you,
    safe to stretch out and help others,
    those troubled in faith,
    those troubled in body.

Father, help us to do with our bodies what we
        proclaim,
    that our faith be known to you
    and to others,
    and be effective in all the world.

MASAI, TANZANIA

FOR THE WONDER OF YOUR LOVE

All glorious God, we give you thanks:
in your Son Jesus Christ you have given us every
    spiritual blessing in the heavenly realms.
You chose us, before the world was made,
    to be your holy people, without fault in your
    sight.
You adopted us as your children in Christ.
You have set us free by his blood,
    you have forgiven our sins.
You have made known to us your secret purpose, to
    bring heaven and earth into unity in Christ.
You have given us your Holy Spirit,
    the seal and pledge of our inheritance.
All praise and glory be yours, O God,
    for the richness of your grace,
    for the splendor of your gifts,
    for the wonder of your love.

INSPIRED BY EPHESIANS 1:3—18

LIFT EVERY VOICE

Lift every voice and sing till earth and heaven
    ring,
ring with the harmonies of liberty.

Let our rejoicing rise high as the listening skies;
let it resound loud as the rolling sea.
Sing a song full of the faith that the dark past has
    taught us;
sing a song full of the hope that the present has
    brought us;
facing the rising sun of our new day begun,
let us march on, till victory is won.

Stony the road we trod, bitter the chastening rod,
felt in the days when hope unborn had died,
yet with a steady beat, have not our weary feet
come to the place for which our parents sighed?
We have come over a way that with tears has been
    watered;
we have come, treading our path through the blood
    of the slaughtered,
out from the gloomy past, till now we stand at
    last
where the white gleam of our bright star is cast.

God of our weary years, God of our silent tears,
thou who hast brought us thus far on the way;
thou who hast by the might led us into the light;
keep us for ever in the path, we pray.
Lest our feet stray from the places, our God, where
    we met thee;
lest, our hearts drunk with the wine of the world,
    we forget thee;

shadowed beneath thy hand may we for ever stand,
true to our God, true to our native land.

AFRICAN-AMERICAN ANTHEM

ONE FAMILY

We offer our thanks to thee
    for sending thy only Son to die for us all.
In a world divided by color bars,
    how sweet a thing it is to know
    that in thee we all belong to one family.

There are times when we,
       unprivileged people,
    weep tears that are not loud but deep,
    when we think of the suffering we experience.
We come to thee, our only hope and refuge.
Help us, O God, to refuse to be embittered
    against those who handle us with harshness.
       We are grateful to thee
    for the gift of laughter at all times.
Save us from hatred of those who oppress us.
May we follow the spirit of thy Son Jesus Christ.

BANTU

THE MOTOR UNDER ME
IS RUNNING HOT

Lord,
the motor under me is running hot.
Lord,
there are twenty-eight people
and lots of luggage in the truck.
Underneath are my bad tires.
The brakes are unreliable.
Unfortunately I have no money,
and parts are difficult to get.
Lord,
I did not overload the truck.
Lord,
"Jesus is mine"
is written on the vehicle,
for without him I would not drive a single mile.
The people in the back are relying on me.
They trust me because they see the words:
"Jesus is mine."
Lord,
I trust you!
First comes the straight road
with little danger,
I can keep my eyes on the women,
children and chickens in the village.
But soon the road begins to turn,

it goes up and down,
it jumps and dances,
this death-road to Kumasi.
Tractors carrying mahogany trunks drive
as if there were no right or left.
Lord,
Kumasi is the temptation
to take more people than we should.
Let's overcome it!
The road to Accra is another problem.
Truck drivers try to beat the record,
although the road is poor
and has many holes
and there are many curves
before we come to the hills.
And finally to Akwasim.
Passing large churches in every village,
I am reminded of you, and in reverence
I take off my hat.
Now downhill in second gear.

GHANA

SUPPLICATION

All we are, all we have, is a gift. God is always more ready to hear and to give than we are to ask and to receive. Jesus taught his disciples to regard God as their Father who long before they had asked knew their needs. It is in the nature of the parent-child relationship for the child to ask, for it is so utterly dependent on its parent. Jesus wanted his followers to have a like trusting relationship, devoid of anxiety and worry. God cared for them, and so if they knocked it would be opened to them, if they asked it would be given to them, if they sought they would find, because the Power that controlled the universe was completely on their side and well-disposed toward them. The resources of this God were available to them. And this was a God who lavished his bounty prodigally on nature, covering the fields with lilies more splendid than King Solomon in all his glory. They were precious to God, for each was known by name; and no harm would befall them, for even the hairs of their heads were numbered. They were of much greater value than any sparrow, which would not fall to the ground without God taking note of the occurrence. If God's concern for inanimate and nonhuman nature was so great, what must it be for us human creatures?

Saint Paul was to exhort his Philippian converts, by words that echoed our Lord's teaching, that we should not be anxious for anything, that we should bring all our needs to God in faith, believing that we did not have to persuade God to be nice to us, for he was always very well disposed toward us.

Saint Julian of Norwich says prayer "is yearning, beseeching and beholding." We are made for God, we yearn to be filled with the fullness of God, and so we come asking the one who is always eager to give. We place ourselves in his hands as suppliants, in the attitude of those who know they have nothing that they have not received, before the One who is ever the gracious one ready to give beyond our asking and our deserving. We are like a parched land thirsty for the gift of rain—*yearning, beeseeching, waiting* and *asking* and assured that we will be heard and that we will be given. For Jesus taught his disciples to pray, "Give us this day our daily bread."

Joseph said to his brothers, "I am Joseph! Can my father be still alive?" They were so dumbfounded at finding themselves face to face with Joseph that they could not answer. Joseph said to them, "Come closer to me," and when they did so, he said, "I am your brother Joseph, whom you sold into Egypt. Now do not be distressed or blame yourselves for selling me into slavery here; it was to save lives that God sent me ahead of you. For there have now been two years of famine in the land, and there will be another five years with neither ploughing nor harvest. God sent me on ahead of you to ensure that you will have descendants on earth, and to preserve for you a host of survivors. It is clear that it was not you who sent me here, but God, and he has made me Pharaoh's chief counselor, lord over his whole household and ruler of all Egypt."

GENESIS 45:3−8

GOD BLESS AFRICA

God bless Africa.
Guard her children.
Guide her rulers,
And give her peace for Jesus Christ's sake. Amen.

TREVOR HUDDLESTON

Trevor Huddleston was an Anglican monk of the Community of the Resurrection, based in Mirfield, England, who sprang to prominence in the 1950s when he allied himself with black South Africans in early resistance to apartheid. He went on to become a bishop in Tanzania and in London and, later, Archbishop of the Indian Ocean.

MAKE US HOLY

Holy Father, make us holy.
Holy Jesus, make us holy.
Holy Spirit, make us holy.
Holy God, make us whole. Amen.

INSTITUTE FOR SPIRITUALITY, CPSA

VICTORY IS OURS

Goodness is stronger than evil;
Love is stronger than hate;
Light is stronger than darkness;
Life is stronger than death;
Victory is ours through Him who loves us.

DESMOND TUTU

Deliver Me

From the cowardice that dare not face new truths,
From the laziness that is contented with half truths,
From the arrogance that thinks it knows all truth,
Good Lord deliver me.

BREAD FOR TOMORROW, KENYA

Nothing Between Us and the Love of God

With all this in mind, what are we to say? If God is on our side, who is against us? He did not spare his own Son, but gave him up for us all; how can he fail to lavish every other gift upon us? Who will bring a charge against those whom God has chosen? Not God, who acquits! Who will pronounce judgment? Not Christ, who died, or rather rose again; not Christ, who is at God's right hand and pleads our cause! Then what can separate us from the love of Christ? Can affliction or hardship? Can persecution, hunger, nakedness, danger, or sword? "We are being done to death for your sake all day long," as scripture says; "we have been treated like sheep for slaughter"—and yet, throughout it all, overwhelming victory is ours through him who loved us. For I am convinced that there is nothing in death or life, in the realm

of spirits or superhuman powers, in the world as it is or
the world as it shall be, in the forces of the universe, in
heights or depths—nothing in all creation that can separate us from the love of God in Christ Jesus our Lord.

ROMANS 8:31–39

The Angels Will Deliver Us

When anyone prays, the angels that minister to God and
watch over mankind gather round about him and join
with him in his prayer. Nor is that all. Every Christian—
each of the "little ones" who are in the Church—has an
angel of his own, who "always beholds the face of our Father which is in heaven" (Matthew 18:10), and who looks
upon the Godhead of the Creator. This angel prays with
us and works with us, as far as he can, to obtain the things
for which we ask.

"The angel of the Lord," so it is written, "encamps
beside those who fear the Lord and delivers them"
(Psalm 33:8), while Jacob speaks of "the angel who delivers me from all evils" (Genesis 48:16): and what he
says is true not of himself only but of all those who set
their trust in God. It would seem, then, that when a
number of the faithful meet together genuinely for the
glory of Christ, since they all fear the Lord, each of them

will have, encamped beside him, his own angel whom God has appointed to guard him and care for him. So, when the saints are assembled, there will be a double Church, one of men and one of angels.

ORIGEN

CHRIST ENOUGH

Who will save our land and people?
Who can rescue us from wrong?
We are lost—faint, false and foolish—
We have slighted God too long.
Save thy people, Lord our Saviour,
Guide us home from country far;
Holy Fire, consume our rancors:
Thy kingdom come—in Africa.

Make our land as clean and wholesome
As the white of sea-washed sands;
Stretch our vision vast and boundless
As our brown-spread, dusty lands.
Make our people strong and steadfast
As the hills that claw our sky;
Hear our prayer for land and people:
"God bless Africa," we cry.

We believe God is our Saviour:
Christ enough to heal our land.
He will use the Church, his servants:
We on earth his stretched-out hand.
May his Church in loving service,
Shown to all whose path is rough,
Give a clear, united witness,
And proclaim: "Christ is enough!"

Christ enough to break all barriers;
Christ enough in peace, in strife;
Christ enough to build our nation;
Christ enough for death, for life;
Christ enough for old and lonely;
Christ enough for those who fall;
Christ enough to save the sin-sick;
Christ enough for one; for all!

JOHN B. GARDENER

John B. Gardener, a schoolteacher, wrote this as a hymn for Methodist missions in South Africa.

GO DOWN, MOSES

When Israel was in Egypt's land,
Let my people go,
Oppressed so hard they could not stand,
Let my people go.

Go down, Moses,
Way down in Egypt land,
Tell de Pharaoh
To let my people go.

Thus saith the Lord, bold Moses said,
Let my people go.
If not I'll smite your firstborn dead,
Let my people go.

No more shall they in bondage toil . . .
Let my people go.
Let them come out with Egypt's spoil . . .
Let my people go.

Oh, 'twas a dark and dismal night . . .
Let my people go.
When Moses led the Israelites . . .
Let my people go.

The Lord told Moses what to do . . .
Let my people go.
To lead the children of Israel through . . .
Let my people go.

As I stood by the waterside . . .
Let my people go.
At the command of God, it did divide . . .
Let my people go.

When they reached the other shore . . .
Let my people go.
They sang a song of triumph o'er . . .
Let my people go.

Pharaoh said he would go across . . .
Let my people go.
But Pharaoh and his host were lost . . .
Let my people go.

Oh, Moses, the cloud shall cleave the way . . .
Let my people go.
A fire by night, a shade by day . . .
Let my people go.

You'll not get lost in the wilderness . . .
Let my people go.
With a lighted candle in your breast . . .
Let my people go.

AFRICAN-AMERICAN SPIRITUAL

TAKE MY HAND, PRECIOUS LORD

Take my hand, Precious Lord,
Lead me on, let me stand.
I am tired, I am weak, I am worn.

Through the storm, through the night, lead me on to
    the light.
Take my hand, Precious Lord, lead me home.

When my way grows drear, Precious Lord, linger
    near
When my life is almost gone.
Hear my cry, hear my call, hold my hand, lest I fall.
Take my hand, Precious Lord, lead me home.

When the darkness appears and the night draws near
And the day is past and gone,
At the river I stand,
Guide my feet, hold my hand.
Take my hand, Precious Lord, lead me home.

THOMAS A. DORSEY

*Thomas A. Dorsey was born near Atlanta, Georgia, in 1899. He started
out his music career in a small jazz band in Chicago, but later went on to
dedicate his life entirely to writing gospel songs. "Precious Lord" was Mar-
tin Luther King, Jr.'s favorite hymn.*

LITANY

My God, my God, why have you forsaken me?
Our God, our God, why have you forsaken us?
My God, our God, my Father, our Father
When will we ever learn, when will they ever
    learn?

Oh when will we ever learn that you intended us
    for
Shalom, for wholeness, for peace,
For fellowship, for togetherness, for brotherhood,
For sisterhood, for family?
When will we ever learn that you created us
As your children
As members of one family
Your family
The human family—
Created us for linking arms
To express our common humanity.

God, my Father
I am filled
With anguish and puzzlement.
Why, oh God, is there so much
Suffering, such needless suffering?
Everywhere we look there is pain
And suffering.
Why must your people in El Salvador,
In Nicaragua,
In Guatemala,
In ....,
In ....,
Why must there be so much killing,
So much death and destruction,
So much bloodshed,
So much suffering,

So much oppression, and injustice, and poverty and
   hunger?

Why, oh why, my God, our God,
My Father, our Father
Why must your people endure all the mindless
   violence
And bloodletting in Ulster, in Ethiopia, in
The Sudan, in Somalia, in Liberia, in Angola, in
Mozambique, in South Africa, in ......,
In ......

Oh God, my God, our God, my Father, our
Father, please is there some explanation
For what is happening in the Lebanon—
Poor Terry Waite and those other hostages—
Can you tell me please why in
The land of the Prince of Peace, why
Should your people suffer so in
Gaza, in the West Bank, in Beit Sahur
From deportations, house demolitions and now
In Tel Aviv from Scuds
Ever fearful of poisoning in chemical warfare?

I don't understand, oh God, my God,
Our God, oh my Father, our Father,
Why, oh why, must there be so much
Pain and suffering in your creation so very good and
   beautiful?

In Sri Lanka, in Calcutta, in Burma, in Kampuchia
Why are there boat people bobbing
About so vulnerably between vile camps in Hong
    Kong and in the deep blue sea, and Viet
    Nam?
And what about Latvia, and Lithuania, and
    Chernobyl?

I am dumbfounded
I am bewildered
And in agony—

This is the world
You loved so much that for it
You gave your only begotten
Son, our Lord and Saviour Jesus Christ, to hang
From the cross, done to death
Love nearly overwhelmed by hate
Light nearly extinguished by darkness
Life nearly destroyed by death—
But not quite—

For love vanquished hate
For life overcame death, there—
Light overwhelmed
Darkness, there—
And we can live with hope.

Now there is the carnage
And devastation in Iraq, in Kuwait, in Saudi Arabia,
    in Tel Aviv.
What am I to make of it all?
Why did Saddam attack and overrun Kuwait?
I don't know—
Why did America
Attack Granada, and go into Panama?
Why did they occupy the West Bank?
I don't know—

All I know, God, is that it's all so horrendous,
The high-tech war with computers
That declare that we are so advanced,
And we can bomb with breathtaking
Precision and people die and
Buildings collapse, and blood flows, whether it
Is precision bombing or—
It is all the same, you are dead.
And in Paris, and New York, and Birmingham,
In Tel Aviv, in Baghdad, in Riyadh
A mother waits anxiously for news
Of her son, of her daughter, of her husband.
A child waits . . .

In the Eucharist as we offer the bread
That bread is all the bewilderment, the anguish, the
    blood, the pain, the injustice,

The poverty, the hate, the anger, the fear, the death,
The war, the bombs—
And we offer it all together with
The perfect all self-sufficient sacrifice
Of the Lamb without blemish
For peace,
For transfiguration, for compassion,
For Bush, for Hussein, for soldiers,
For civilians, for peace, for Shalom,
For family, for togetherness—

Oh my God, our God, oh my Father
When will we ever learn?
When will they ever learn?

DESMOND TUTU

MAY GOD AGREE WITH US

May God agree with us.
Yes, my God, you will save us:
yes, my God, you will guide us,
and your thoughts will be with us night and day.
Grant us to remain a long time,
like the great wing of rain, like the long rains.
Give us the fragrance of a purifying branch.

Be the support of our burdens,
and may they always be untied,
the shells of fertility and mothers and children.
God be our safeguard, also where the shepherds are.
God, sky, with stars at your sides
and the moon in the middle of your stomach,
morning of my God that is rising,
come and hit us with your waters.
And God said: "All right."

SAMBURU, KENYA

MAKE US INSTRUMENTS OF
YOUR FAITH

For your blessing we thank you, God: faith in you.
Increase it, we beg, so that we no longer doubt.
Drive out all our miserliness, so that we do not
    refuse you anything.
Increase our faith, for the sake of those without faith.
Make us instruments of your faith, for those with
    only a little.
Fill our bodies with faith, our bodies that work for
    you all our days.
Help us to avoid the enemies of our faith, or to
    overcome them.

You are with us in confrontations; this we believe.
In your hands we place ourselves, and are secure.
Make haste to enter our hearts; make haste.

MASAI, TANZANIA

I HAVE NO OTHER HELPER
THAN YOU

I have no other helper than you,
no other father,
no other redeemer,
no other support.
I pray to you.
Only you can help me.
My present misery
is too great.
Despair grips me,
and I am at my wits' end.
I am sunk in the depths,
and I cannot pull myself up
or out.
If it is your will,
help me out of this misery.
Let me know
that you are stronger
than all misery and all enemies.

O Lord, if I come through this,
please let the experience
contribute to my and my brothers' blessing.
You will not forsake me;
this I know.
Amen.

GHANA

GRANT ME TO WALK ALL ROADS

My God, grant me to walk all roads.
My God, cover me with your cloak.
My God, make me be covered by the black cloak
    softened by oil.
My God, hold me tight when I walk
    and when I stand still.
My God, do not throw me out of you.
My God, keep me in your stomach.
My God, guard me; God, answer me.
My God, do not throw me away.
Listen, that we may agree on what I am telling you.
Grant us a life that never ends,
like the one we live.
God, answer with favor
to what we told you.

SAMBURU, KENYA

Be for Us a Moon of Joy

May you be for us a moon of joy and happiness. Let the young become strong and the grown man maintain his strength, the pregnant woman be delivered and the woman who has given birth suckle her child. Let the stranger come to the end of his journey and those who remain at home dwell safely in their houses. Let the flocks that go to feed in the pastures return happily. May you be a moon of harvest and of calves. May you be a moon of restoration and of good health.

MENSA, ETHIOPIA

The Privilege Is Ours to Share in the Loving

Almighty God, our heavenly Father, the privilege is ours to share in the loving, healing, reconciling mission of your Son Jesus Christ, our Lord, in this age and wherever we are. Since without you we can do no good thing.

May your Spirit make us wise;

May your Spirit guide us;

May your Spirit renew us;

May your Spirit strengthen us;

So that we will be:

Strong in faith,
Discerning in proclamation,
Courageous in witness,
Persistent in good deeds.
This we ask through the name of the Father.

CHURCH OF THE PROVINCE OF THE WEST INDIES

WE ARE YOUR CHILDREN

Father, we are your children, your Spirit lives in us and
we are in your Spirit: hear us, for it is your Spirit who
speaks through us as we pray.
Lord hear us.

Father, you created the heavens and the earth: bless the
produce of our land and the works of our hands.
Lord hear us.

Father, you created us in your own image: teach us to
honor you in all your children.
Lord hear us.

Father, in your steadfast love you provide for your creation: grant good rains for our crops.
Lord hear us.

Father, you inspired the prophets of old: grant that your Church may faithfully proclaim your truth to the world.
Lord hear us.

Father, you sent your Son into the world: reveal him to others through his life in us.
Lord hear us.

Lord Jesus, you sent your apostles to make disciples of all nations: bless the bishops of this province, especially *N* our bishop, together with *N* our metropolitan, and all other ministers of your Church.
Christ hear us.

Lord Jesus, for your sake men and women forsook all and followed you: call many to serve you in religious communities and in the ordained ministry of your Church.
Christ hear us.

Lord Jesus, you called your disciples to take up the cross: deepen in each of us a sense of vocation.
Christ hear us.

You prayed for your Church to be one: unite all Christians that the world may believe.
Christ hear us.

You forgave the thief on the cross: bring us all to penitence and reconciliation.
Christ hear us.

You broke down the walls that divide us: bring the people of this world to live in peace and concord.
Christ hear us.

You taught us through Paul, your apostle, to pray for kings and rulers: bless and guide all who are in authority.
Christ hear us.

You were rich yet for our sake you became poor: move those who have wealth to share generously with those who are poor.
Christ hear us.

You sat among the learned, listening and asking them questions: inspire all who teach and all who learn.
Christ hear us.

You cured by your healing touch and word: heal the sick and bless those who minister to them.
Christ hear us.

You were unjustly condemned by Pontius Pilate: strengthen our brothers and sisters who are suffering injustice and persecution.
Christ hear us.

You lived as an exile in Egypt: protect and comfort all refugees.
Christ hear us.

You knew the love and care of an earthly home: be with migrant workers and protect their families.
Christ hear us.

You open and none can shut: open the gates of your kingdom to those who have died without hearing your gospel.
Christ hear us.

You have been glorified in the lives of innumerable saints: give us strength through their prayers to follow in their footsteps.
Christ hear us.

Father, we know that you are good and that you hear those who call upon you: give to us and to all people what is best for us, that we may glorify you through your Son, Jesus Christ our Lord, who is alive and reigns with you and the Holy Spirit, one God, now and for ever.
Amen.

AN ANGLICAN PRAYER BOOK 1989
CHURCH OF THE PROVINCE OF SOUTHERN AFRICA

PRAYER OF A DYING MAN

And though I behold a man hate me,
I will love him.
O God, Father, help me, Father!
O God, Creator, help me, Father!
And even though I behold a man hate me,
I will love him.

DINKA, SUDAN

A PRAYER FOR AFRICA

O Lord, O Ruler of the world,
O Creator, O Father,
this prayer is for Africa.
For our brothers in the South,
for our brothers in the North.
You know
that the white brothers have made their black
    brothers
second-class people.
O Lord, this hurts us so much.
We suffer from this.
You have given us a dark skin
so that we may better bear
your strong sun.

Why have our brothers done this to us?
They are not better than we,
and we are not better than they.
What comforts us is
that you always love most
those who suffer most.
We call ourselves Christians on both sides.
But we go to different churches,
as if there were also different heavens.
The white men
still have power in parts of Africa.
Help them to use their power wisely
and accept us as brothers.
Take the mistrust out of their hearts and minds
and make them share with us,
for this is our continent,
or, more truly, yours;
and you have marked us for this continent
and them for the North.
We also pray for ourselves.
O Lord,
keep our hearts free from hatred.
And let us also be grateful for what
missionaries have done here
and others too, for government and for the
      economy.
Let us become brothers again,
as it should be among your children.
You have died for all,

and risen,
Halleluia!
We praise you, our Father,
who are greater than Europe and Africa;
who love where we hate;
who long ago could have destroyed us.
But you love us so much
and we have not deserved it.
Praise be to you, O Lord!
Amen.

GHANA

I ABANDON MYSELF TO YOU

My Father, I abandon myself to you. Do with me as
    you will.
Whatever you may do with me, I thank you.
I am prepared for anything, I accept everything.
Provided your will is fulfilled in me and in all
creatures I ask for nothing more, my God.
I place my soul in your hands.
I give it to you, my God,
with all the love of my heart
because I love you.
And for me it is a necessity of love,
this gift of myself,
this placing of myself in your hands

without reserve
in boundless confidence
because you are my Father.

CHARLES DE FOUCAULD

Charles de Foucauld, French by birth, found his vocation as a Christian in the deserts of North Africa. He sought to incarnate the Gospel by living among the Bedouin without seeking to convert them by preaching. His spirituality gave birth to the Fraternities of the Little Sisters and Brothers of Jesus.

DELIVER US FROM FEAR OF THE UNKNOWN

O Lord, we beseech thee to deliver us from the fear of the unknown future; from fear of failure; from fear of poverty; from fear of bereavement; from fear of loneliness; from fear of sickness and pain; from fear of age; and from fear of death. Help us, O Father, by thy grace to love and fear thee only, fill our hearts with cheerful courage and loving trust in thee; through our Lord and Master Jesus Christ.

AKANU IBAIM, NIGERIA

We Kneel Before Thee

O thou Chief of Chiefs, we kneel before thee in obeisance and adoration. Like the bird in the branches, we praise thy heavenly glory. Like the village sharpening stone, thou art always available and never exhausted. Remove, we pray thee, our sins that hide thy face. Thou knowest that we are poor and unlearned; that we often work when hungry. Send rain in due season for our gardens that our food may not fail. Protect us from the cold and danger by night. Help us to keep in health that we may rejoice in strength. May our villages be filled with children. Emancipate us from the fear of the fetish and the witch doctor and from all manner of superstitions. Save the people, especially the Christian boys and girls in the villages, from the evil that surrounds them. All this we ask in the name of Jesus Christ thy Son.

ZAIRE

Your Holy Spirit Blows Over This Earth

On your last days on earth
you promised
to leave us the Holy Spirit
as our present comforter.

We also know that your Holy Spirit blows over this
   earth.
But we do not understand him.
Many think
he is only wind or a feeling.
Let your Holy Spirit
break into our lives.
Let him come like blood into our veins,
so that we will be driven
entirely by your will.
Let your Spirit
blow over wealthy Europe and America,
so that men there will be humble.
Let him blow over the poor parts of the world,
so that men there need suffer no more.
Let him blow over Africa,
so that men here may understand
what true freedom is.
There are a thousand voices and spirits
in this world,
but we want to hear only your voice,
and be open only to your Spirit.

GHANA

THE RAINBOW OF THY PEACE

O bless this people, Lord, who seek their own face
under the mask and can hardly recognize it. . . .

O bless this people that breaks its bond . . .

And with them, all the peoples of Europe,
All the peoples of Asia,
All the peoples of Africa,
All the peoples of America,
Who sweat blood and sufferings.

And see, in the midst of these millions of waves,
The sea swell of the heads of my people.
And grant to their warm hands that they may clasp
The earth in a girdle of brotherly hands,
Beneath the rainbow of thy peace.

LEOPOLD SEDAR SENGHOR

Leopold Sedar Senghor was a noted French poet and essayist and was president of Senegal, West Africa, in the 1960s.

BE NOT AFRAID

But now, Jacob, this is the word
    of the Lord,
the word of your Creator,

of him who fashioned you, Israel:
Have no fear, for I have redeemed
    you;
I call you by name; you are mine.
When you pass through water I shall
    be with you;
when you pass through rivers they
    will not overwhelm you;
walk through fire, and you will not
    be scorched,
through flames, and they will not
    burn you.

ISAIAH 43 : 1 — 2

I SHALL NOT FORGET YOU

But Zion says,
"The Lord has forsaken me;
my Lord has forgotten me."
Can a woman forget the infant at her
    breast,
or a mother the child of her womb?
But should even these forget,
I shall never forget you.
I have inscribed you on the palms of
    my hands;

your walls are always before my
eyes.

ISAIAH 49:14–16

ANSWER OF A STARVING CHILD . . .
"WHO IS JESUS CHRIST?"

The answer of a starving child in Ghana:
"Oh! Jesus. I have heard of that name. You say he is
the Life of the world. Life! But I am hungry. I am lifeless.
There is no milk in my mother's breasts. She is sick and
weak. They tell me that some people called "Red Cross"
are sending or have sent some powdered milk. But I am
hungry. I am dying. You say Jesus is the Life of the World?
But I am dying. Can Jesus help to keep me alive?"

AN AFRICAN CALL FOR LIFE

A SOUTH AFRICAN REPLY

"Life is terrible here, Jesus. It is not the full life you came
to bring. You are weak, Jesus. We would prefer a more
powerful Jesus to save us from the oppression inflicted
upon us by the White Boers. They say that we are black,

therefore, we must live apart from them. Yes, Jesus, we believe that you are the Son of God, but you are too weak. Bishop Desmond Tutu says that it is just a matter of time. Yes, but when? When?"

An African Call for Life

A Woman's Answer

"Yes, Jesus, I accept that you are the Life of the world, but we women are oppressed by men. They ask, "can a woman also be called to the ordained ministry of the Church?" Oh, Jesus, why do you favor men, your church is male-dominated. I have to change my name into a man's after marriage. He believes that I am inferior. He only accepts me out of pity. Yes, Jesus, the Life of the world, make life better for us, women."

An African Call for Life

Reflections on Wholeness

Busy, normal people: the world is here.
Can you hear it wailing, crying, whispering?
Listen: the world is here.

Don't you hear it,
Praying and sighing and groaning for wholeness?
Sighing and whispering: wholeness,
wholeness, wholeness?
An arduous, tiresome, difficult journey
towards wholeness.
God, who gives us strength of
body, make us whole.
Wholeness of persons: well-being of individuals.
The cry for bodily health and spiritual
strength is echoed from person to
person, from patient to doctor.
It goes out from a soul to its pastor.
We, busy, "normal" people: we are sick.
We yearn to experience wholeness in
our innermost being:
In health and prosperity, we continue
to feel un-well,
Un-fulfilled, or half-filled.
There is a hollowness in our pretended
well-being:
Our spirits cry out for the well-being of
the whole human family.
We pride ourselves in our traditional
communal ideology, our extended family.
The beggars and the mad people in our streets:
—Where are their relatives?
Who is their father? Where is their mother?
We cry for the wholeness of humanity.

But the litany of brokenness is without end.
Black and white;
Rich and poor;
Hausa and Yomba;
Presbyterian and Roman Catholic:
We are all parts of each other,
We yearn to be folded into the fullness
of life—together.
Life, together with the outcast,
The prisoner, the mad woman,
the abandoned child;
Our wholeness is intertwined with their hurt.
Wholeness means healing the hurt,
Working with Christ to heal the hurt,
Seeing and feeling the suffering of others,
Standing alongside them.
Their loss of dignity is not their loss:
It is the loss of our human dignity,
We busy, "normal" people.
The person next to you: with a different
language and culture,
With a different skin or hair color—
It is God's diversity, making an unbroken
rainbow circle—
Our covenant of peace with God, encircling
the whole of humanity.
Christians have to re-enact the miracle
of Good Friday:
The torn veil, the broken walls, the

bridge over the chasm,
The broken wall of hostility between
the Jew and the Gentile.
The wall between sacred and secular?
There is no wall
There is only God at work in the whole;
Heal the sores on the feet;
Salvage the disintegrated personality;
Bind the person back into the whole.
For without that one, we do not have a whole.
Even if there are ninety-nine:
Without that one, we do not have a whole.
God, who gives us strength of
body, make us whole.

AN AFRICAN CALL FOR LIFE

DAILY LIFE

Is it not wonderful that God is forever breathing his breath into us? The Christian God is not as the deists conceived him—someone who as it were wound up the clockwork of the universe and then left it all to its own devices, now and again having to intervene to wind it up again when it was running down. No, God created and God continues to create, to uphold everything in existence, for if God were to forget us even for a split second, then we, everything, would all disintegrate into the nothingness, the oblivion out of which God's creative fiat called us into existence. God in the second story of creation made Adam out of dust and animated him by blowing God's own breath into his nostrils. And, to keep him in being, God has to do that from moment to every single moment. Julian of Norwich saw in a vision all that God had created nestling in the palm of God's hand, and it was in size like a hazelnut. And it was maintained in existence by the selfsame love that had brought it into being. That is how intimate our relationship with God is, whether we acknowledge it as such or not.

Consequently, nothing that is important for us can be of no concern to God. Our natural ambience is the divine, and so Teilhard de Chardin could speak of what he called *le milieu divin*. We are always in the presence of God. Prayer is acknowledging that we are in that presence. And so we place ourselves in that presence in the morning, committing all we are and all we shall do that day into God's hands and in utter reliance on him, praying for safety and security and a blessing on what we shall undertake, seeking to discover God's will for us and the grace to perform it. Nothing is insignificant for God that is important for us. This is a tremendous assertion. We thank him for the night's rest and for protection in the dark hours when evil is about. And when night falls we thank God for all that has been in the day past, and commend ourselves into his safekeeping.

How deeply God loves us, asking nothing in return except the gift of loving hearts.

Saint Augustine said about God:

All that he is and all that he has, he gives;
All that we are, and all that we have, he asks!

After they had gone, an angel of the Lord appeared to Joseph in a dream, and said, "Get up, take the child and his mother and escape with them to Egypt, and stay there until I tell you; for Herod is going to search for the child to kill him."

So Joseph got up, took mother and child by night, and sought refuge with them in Egypt, where he stayed till Herod's death. This was to fulfill what the Lord had declared through the prophet: "Out of Egypt I have called my son."

MATTHEW 2:13–15

YOU HAVE PREPARED IN PEACE THE PATH

O God, you have prepared in peace the path I must follow today. Help me to walk straight on that path. If I speak, remove lies from my lips. If I am hungry, take away from me all complaint. If I have plenty, destroy pride in me. May I go through the day calling on you, you, O Lord, who know no other Lord.

GALLA, ETHIOPIA

O SUN, AS YOU RISE IN THE EAST

O sun, as you rise in the east through God's
    leadership,
wash away all evils of which I have thought
    throughout the night.
Bless me, so that my enemies will not kill me and my
    family;
guide me through hard work.
O God, give me mercy upon our children who are
    suffering;
bring riches today as the sun rises;
bring all fortunes to me today.

ABALUYIA, KENYA

OUR HEART IS RESTLESS

Thou awakest us to delight in thy praises; for thou
madest us for thyself, and our heart is restless, until it re-
pose in thee.

SAINT AUGUSTINE

A MORNING PRAYER

O God, you have let me pass the night in peace,
let me pass the day in peace.
Wherever I may go upon my way
which you made peaceable for me,
O God, lead my steps.
When I have spoken, keep lies away from me.
When I am hungry, keep me from murmuring.
When I am satisfied, keep me from pride.
Calling upon you, I pass the day,
O Lord, who has no Lord.

BORAN, KENYA

AN EVENING PRAYER

O God, you have let me pass this day in peace,
let me pass the night in peace
O Lord who has no Lord,
there is no strength but in thee.
Thou alone hast no obligation.
Under thy hand I pass the night.
Thou art my mother and my father.

BORAN, KENYA

COVER ME WITH THE NIGHT

Come, Lord,
and cover me with the night.
Spread your grace over us
as you assured us you would do.

Your promises are more than
all the stars in the sky;
your mercy is deeper than the night.
Lord, it will be cold.
The night comes with its breath of death.
Night comes; the end comes; you come.

Lord, we wait for you
day and night.

GHANA

THE SUN HAS DISAPPEARED

The sun has disappeared.
I have switched off the light,
and my wife and children are asleep.
The animals in the forest are full of fear,
and so are the people on their mats.
They prefer the day with your sun
to the night.

But I still know that your moon is there,
and your eyes and also your hands.
Thus I am not afraid.
This day again
you led us wonderfully.
Everybody went to his mat
satisfied and full.
Renew us during our sleep,
that in the morning
we may come afresh to our daily jobs.
Be with our brothers far away in Asia
who may be getting up now. Amen.

GHANA

NIGHT SILENCE

Lord of light
help me to know
that you are also
Lord of night.

And by your choice
when all is dark
and still and stark
you use your voice.

HARRY ALFRED WIGGETT

THE SILENT SELF

Silence is
    sitting still
    standing still
    lying still
consciously
    gratefully
        gracefully
breathing
inspiring—
    being inspired with life
               and love
    from him from whom these
        gifts do come—
the Lord of life and love—
the living Lord Jesus.

And in the stillness
        knowing
    and joyfully acknowledging
    that in Jesus alone
the silence of life and love is found.

Then to humbly rest
      sit
    stand
    lie
to bow the knee

in all that satisfying silence—
     and be fulfilled.

HARRY ALFRED WIGGETT

SEED SILENCE

I did not hear you fall
from pod to mother earth.

I did not hear you call
or cry your humble birth.

I did not hear you sigh
as silently you grew.

I did not hear a Why
because God made you you.

And yet your silence spoke
of confidence and might

and purpose as you broke
through earth into the light.

HARRY ALFRED WIGGETT

FOR THE LIVING DEAD

O good and innocent dead, hear us: hear us, you guiding, all-knowing ancestors, you are neither blind nor deaf to this life we live: you did yourselves once share it. Help us therefore for the sake of our devotion, and for our good.

MENDE, SIERRA LEONE

FOR A DISOBEDIENT SON

O God, thou knowest this is my son; I begat him and trained him and labored for him, and now that he should do some work for me, he refuses. In anything he does now in the world may he not prosper, until he comes back to me and begs my pardon.

MENDE, SIERRA LEONE

FOR A REPENTANT SON

O God, this is my son; he left me without any good fortune in the world because he knows I have cursed him; he has now to beg me to pull the curse as I am pulling now. Wherever he goes now may he prosper and have many children.

MENDE, SIERRA LEONE

A FISHERMAN'S PRAYER

O river, I beg leave to take fish from thee, as my ancestors did before me.

The antelope leaps and its young learns not to climb.

In such a manner the sons of men do as their fathers did.

O river, rise up, engulf your sharp-toothed monsters, and permit our young men to enter the water and enjoy themselves with the fish without being harmed.

If there is acceptance from you, then show it by accepting this baby chick. If not, if you cannot control the monsters, if one of them should harm our sons, then show it by refusing to accept this baby chick.

LOBI, COTE D'IVOIRE

GOD FREE YOU

May God free you, may God guard you night and
    day.
May God set you in your right place, and may you
    spread out like the grass of a prairie.
Spread out like palm leaves; continue your walk,
and may life be with you.
May God place you where God's stars are placed
    at dawn and at night.
Spread out like water of a lake.
Be numerous like the feet of a millipede.

SAMBURU, KENYA

A BLESSING

May God raise you up
above everything.
Spread out like water of a lake.
Be abundance that never ends,
that never changes.
Be like a mountain.
Be like a camel.
Be like a cloud—
a cloud that brings rain always.
And God promised that it would be so.

SAMBURU, KENYA

Blessing a New House

May the person who is going to live in this house have many children; may he be rich; may he be honest to people and good to the poor; may he not suffer from disease or any other kind of trouble; may he be safe all these years.

NYOLA, KENYA

A Fire Blessing

Thank you, Father, for your free gift of fire.
Because it is through fire that you draw near to us
    every day.
It is with fire that you constantly bless us.
Our Father, bless this fire today.
With your power enter into it.
Make this fire a worthy thing.
A thing that carries your blessing.
Let it become a reminder of your love.
A reminder of life without end.
Make the life of these people to be baptized like this
    fire.
A thing that shines for the sake of people.
A thing that shines for your sake.
Father, heed this sweet-smelling smoke.

Make their life also sweet smelling.
A thing sweet smelling that rises to God.
A holy thing.
A thing fitting for you.

MASAI, TANZANIA

LIGHT A HOLY FIRE

Receive this holy fire.
Make your lives like this fire.
A holy life that is seen.
A life of God that is seen.
A life that has no end.
A life that darkness does not overcome.
May this light of God in you grow.
Light a fire that is worthy of your heads.
Light a fire that is worthy of your children.
Light a fire that is worthy of your fathers.
Light a fire that is worthy of your mothers.
Light a fire that is worthy of God.
Now go in peace.
May the Almighty protect you
today and all days.

MASAI, TANZANIA

THE TIME OF HARVEST IS OVER

The time of harvest is over;
you have given us good crops;
we are going into the bush.
Now I call on you,
so that no evil falls on us
and our feet do not step on anything bad,
and that we meet nothing but good things
and that nothing bad touches us:
you guaranteed these things
and have kept your promise.
May the animals in the bush come to meet us;
let them come within our circle.
Let our arrows not miss them;
let our arrows kill them.
Let the arrows not kill any of us.
You who have given such a good harvest,
continue to walk before us
as you have been doing for our grandparents.

BETAMMARIBE (SOMBA), DAHOMEY (BENIN)

YOU ARE ABOVE, I AM BELOW

Good God of this earth, my Lord,
you are above me, I am below.

When misfortune comes to me,
just as the trees keep off the sun from me
so may you take away misfortune.
My Lord, be my shadow.

Calling on you, I pass the day;
calling on you, I pass the night.
When the moon rises, do not forget me;
when I rise, I do not forget you.
Let the danger pass me by:
God, my Lord, you sun with thirty rays.

God, you hold the bad and the good in your hand;
my Lord, do not allow us to be killed,
we, your little ones, are praying to you.
A person who doesn't know the difference between
    good and bad cannot make you angry;
once he does know and is unwilling to behave
    accordingly,
this is wicked—treat him as you think fit.

God, you made all the animals and people
that live upon the earth;
also, the corn on the earth where we live—
you made that too; we have not made it.
You have given us strength.
You have given us cattle and corn.

We worked the land and the seed grew up for us.
People were satisfied
with the corn which you allowed to grow for us.
The corn in the house has been burned up;
who has burned the corn in the house?
You know who it was.

You have allowed all this to be done;
why have you done this?
You know.
You show before our eyes
the corn which you allowed to grow.
The hungry look at it and are comforted.

When the corn blooms you send butterflies
and locusts into it——locusts and doves.
All this comes from your hand.
Have you caused this to happen?
Why have you done this?
You know why.

If you love me
set me free, I beg you from my heart;
if I do not pray to you from my heart
you do not hear me.
If I pray to you with my heart,
you know it and you are kind to me.

BORAN, KENYA

Let Us Behave Gently

Let us behave gently,
that we may die peacefully;
That our children may stretch out their hands
upon us in burial.

YORUBA, NIGERIA

Turn Your Ear to Hear Me

O God, turn your ear to hear me. Protect my children and my cattle, and even if you are weary, please be patient and listen to my prayer. Under the dark cloak of night, the splendor of your world sleeps on, invisible to us. And when your sun moves across the sky each day, I continue to pray to you. May the spirits of our departed ancestors, who can still exercise their influence on us, keep guard over us, from their places beyond the earth.

NANDI, KENYA

WISDOM

Wisdom is the finest beauty of a person.
Money does not prevent you from becoming blind.
Money does not prevent you from becoming mad.
Money does not prevent you from becoming lame.
You may be ill in any part of your body, so it is
    better for you to go and think again
and to select wisdom.
Come and sacrifice, that you may have rest in your
    body,
inside and outside.

TRADITIONAL AFRICAN

LATE HAVE I LOVED THEE

Late have I loved thee, O Beauty so ancient and so new;
late have I loved thee: for behold thou wert within me,
and I outside; and I sought thee outside and in my unlove-
liness fell upon those lovely things that thou hast made.
Thou wert with me, and I was not with thee. I was kept
from thee by those things, yet had they not been in thee,
they would not have been at all. Thou didst call and cry
to me to break open my deafness: and thou didst send
forth thy beams and shine upon me and chase away my
blindness: thou didst breathe fragrance upon me, and I

drew in my breath and do now pant for thee: I tasted thee, and now hunger and thirst for thee: thou didst touch me, and I have burned for thy peace.

SAINT AUGUSTINE

GRANT ME TO KNOW THEE

Grant me, even me, my dearest Lord, to know thee, and love thee, and rejoice in thee. And if I cannot do these perfectly in this life, let me at least advance to higher degrees every day, till I can come to do them in perfection. Let the knowledge of thee increase in me here, that it may be full hereafter. Let the love of thee grow every day more and more here, that it may be perfect hereafter; that my joy may be great in itself, and full in thee. I know, O God, that thou art a God of truth. Oh, make good thy gracious promises to me, that my joy may be full. Amen.

SAINT AUGUSTINE

Now I Love Thee Alone

Now I love thee alone.
Thee alone do I follow.
Thee alone do I seek.
Thee alone am I ready to serve.
For thou alone hast just dominion.
Under thy sway I long to be.

SAINT AUGUSTINE

This Only Do I Ask

This only do I ask of thy extreme kindness.
That thou convert me wholly to thee
And thou allow nothing to prevent me
from wending my way to thee.

SAINT AUGUSTINE

APPRECIATION

Canon Rowan Smith and Stephen Middelkoop helped me greatly in compiling this anthology, and Doubleday gave me a splendid publisher in Tom Cahill and a splendid editor in Trace Murphy. I am grateful for all that Lynn Franklin, my literary agent, has done. It is a joy to acknowledge my indebtedness to all these wonderful people.

Desmond Tutu, recipient of the Nobel Peace Prize in 1984, retired as Archbishop of Cape Town, South Africa, in 1996. President Nelson Mandela then named him as Chairman of the Truth and Reconciliation Commission, the organization charged with bringing to light the atrocities of apartheid in South Africa and achieving reconciliation with the former oppressors. He is active as a lecturer throughout the world.